Contents

AWARD WINNING SOFT CHOCOLATE CHIP COOKIES

Servings: 72 | Prep: 15m | Cooks: 12m | Total: 1h40m

NUTRITION FACTS

Calories: 177 | Carbohydrates: 20.7g | Fat: 10.5g | Protein: 2.1g | Cholesterol: 24mg

INGREDIENTS

- 4 1/2 cups all-purpose flour
- 2 (3.4 ounce) packages instant vanilla pudding mix
- 2 teaspoons baking soda
- 4 eggs
- 2 cups butter, softened
- 2 teaspoons vanilla extract
- 1 1/2 cups packed brown sugar
- 4 cups semisweet chocolate chips
- 1/2 cup white sugar
- 2 cups chopped walnuts (optional)

DIRECTIONS

1. Preheat oven to 350 degrees F (175 degrees C). Sift together the flour and baking soda, set aside.
2. In a large bowl, cream together the butter, brown sugar, and white sugar. Beat in the instant pudding mix until blended. Stir in the eggs and vanilla. Blend in the flour mixture. Finally, stir in the chocolate chips and nuts. Drop cookies by rounded spoonfuls onto ungreased cookie sheets.
3. Bake for 10 to 12 minutes in the preheated oven. Edges should be golden brown.

THE BEST ROLLED SUGAR COOKIES

Servings: 60| Prep: 20m | Cooks: 8m | Total: 3h | Additional: 2h30m

NUTRITION FACTS

Calories: 109 | Carbohydrates: 14.7g | Fat: 5g | Protein: 1.5g | Cholesterol: 25mg

INGREDIENTS

- 1 1/2 cups butter, softened
- 5 cups all-purpose flour
- 2 cups white sugar
- 2 teaspoons baking powder
- 4 eggs
- 1 teaspoon salt
- 1 teaspoon vanilla extract

DIRECTIONS

1. In a large bowl, cream together butter and sugar until smooth. Beat in eggs and vanilla. Stir in the flour, baking powder, and salt. Cover, and chill dough for at least one hour (or overnight).
2. Preheat oven to 400 degrees F (200 degrees C). Roll out dough on floured surface 1/4 to 1/2 inch thick. Cut into shapes with any cookie cutter. Place cookies 1 inch apart on ungreased cookie sheets.
3. Bake 6 to 8 minutes in preheated oven. Cool completely.

EASY SUGAR COOKIES

Servings: 48 | Prep: 15m | Cooks: 10m | Total: 25m

NUTRITION FACTS

Calories: 86 | Carbohydrates: 11.7g | Fat: 4g | Protein: 0.9g | Cholesterol: 14mg

INGREDIENTS

- 2 3/4 cups all-purpose flour
- 1 1/2 cups white sugar
- 1 teaspoon baking soda
- 1 egg
- 1/2 teaspoon baking powder
- 1 teaspoon vanilla extract
- 1 cup butter, softened

DIRECTIONS

1. Preheat oven to 375 degrees F (190 degrees C). In a small bowl, stir together flour, baking soda, and baking powder. Set aside.
2. In a large bowl, cream together the butter and sugar until smooth. Beat in egg and vanilla. Gradually blend in the dry ingredients. Roll rounded teaspoonfuls of dough into balls, and place onto ungreased cookie sheets.
3. Bake 8 to 10 minutes in the preheated oven, or until golden. Let stand on cookie sheet two minutes before removing to cool on wire racks.

BIG SOFT GINGER COOKIES

Servings: 24 | Prep: 15m | Cooks: 10m | Total: 50m | Additional: 25m

NUTRITION FACTS

Calories: 143 | Carbohydrates: 21.1g | Fat: 6g | Protein: 1.6g | Cholesterol: 8mg

INGREDIENTS

- 2 1/4 cups all-purpose flour
- 3/4 cup margarine, softened
- 2 teaspoons ground ginger
- 1 cup white sugar
- 1 teaspoon baking soda
- 1 egg
- 3/4 teaspoon ground cinnamon
- 1 tablespoon water
- 1/2 teaspoon ground cloves
- 1/4 cup molasses
- 1/4 teaspoon salt
- 2 tablespoons white sugar

DIRECTIONS

1. Preheat oven to 350 degrees F (175 degrees C). Sift together the flour, ginger, baking soda, cinnamon, cloves, and salt. Set aside.
2. In a large bowl, cream together the margarine and 1 cup sugar until light and fluffy. Beat in the egg, then stir in the water and molasses. Gradually stir the sifted ingredients into the molasses mixture. Shape dough into walnut sized balls, and roll them in the remaining 2 tablespoons of sugar. Place the cookies 2 inches apart onto an ungreased cookie sheet, and flatten slightly.
3. Bake for 8 to 10 minutes in the preheated oven. Allow cookies to cool on baking sheet for 5 minutes before removing to a wire rack to cool completely. Store in an airtight container.

BETH'S SPICY OATMEAL RAISIN COOKIES
Servings: 36 | Prep: 15m | Cooks: 12m | Total: 50m | Additional: 23m

NUTRITION FACTS

Calories: 144 | Carbohydrates: 20.6g | Fat: 6.3g | Protein: 1.9g | Cholesterol: 17mg

INGREDIENTS

- 1/2 cup butter, softened
- 1 teaspoon baking soda
- 1/2 cup butter flavored shortening
- 1 teaspoon ground cinnamon
- 1 cup packed light brown sugar
- 1/2 teaspoon ground cloves
- 1/2 cup white sugar
- 1/2 teaspoon salt
- 2 eggs
- 3 cups rolled oats

- 1 teaspoon vanilla extract
- 1 cup raisins
- 1 1/2 cups all-purpose flour

DIRECTIONS

1. Preheat oven to 350 degrees F (175 degrees C).
2. In a large bowl, cream together the butter, butter flavored shortening, brown sugar, white sugar, eggs, and vanilla until smooth. Combine the flour, baking soda, cinnamon, cloves, and salt; stir into the sugar mixture. Stir in the oats and raisins. Drop by rounded teaspoonfuls onto ungreased cookie sheets.
3. Bake 10 to 12 minutes until light and golden. Do not overbake. Let them cool for 2 minutes before removing from cookie sheets to cool completely. Store in airtight container. Make sure you get some, because they don't last long.

BROOKE'S BEST BOMBSHELL BROWNIES

Servings: 24 | Prep: 15m | Cooks: 35m | Total: 50m

NUTRITION FACTS

Calories: 248 | Carbohydrates: 37.5g | Fat: 11.2g | Protein: 2.9g | Cholesterol: 51mg

INGREDIENTS

- 1 cup butter, melted
- 1 1/2 cups all-purpose flour
- 3 cups white sugar
- 1 cup unsweetened cocoa powder
- 1 tablespoon vanilla extract
- 1 teaspoon salt
- 4 eggs
- 1 cup semisweet chocolate chips

DIRECTIONS

1. Preheat oven to 350 degrees F (175 degrees C). Lightly grease a 9x13 baking dish.
2. Combine the melted butter, sugar, and vanilla in a large bowl. Beat in the eggs, one at a time, mixing well after each, until thoroughly blended.
3. Sift the flour, cocoa powder, and salt in a bowl. Gradually stir flour mixture into the egg mixture until blended. Stir in the chocolate morsels. Spread the batter evenly into the prepared baking dish.
4. Bake in preheated oven until an inserted toothpick comes out clean, 35 to 40 minutes. Remove, and cool pan on wire rack before cutting.

ICED PUMPKIN COOKIES

Servings: 36 | Prep: 20m | Cooks: 20m | Total: 1h20m | Additional: 40m

NUTRITION FACTS

Calories: 122 | Carbohydrates: 22.4g | Fat: 3.2g | Protein: 1.2g | Cholesterol: 13mg

INGREDIENTS

- 2 1/2 cups all-purpose flour
- 1 1/2 cups white sugar
- 1 teaspoon baking powder
- 1 cup canned pumpkin puree
- 1 teaspoon baking soda
- 1 egg
- 2 teaspoons ground cinnamon
- 1 teaspoon vanilla extract
- 1/2 teaspoon ground nutmeg
- 2 cups confectioners' sugar
- 1/2 teaspoon ground cloves
- 3 tablespoons milk
- 1/2 teaspoon salt
- 1 tablespoon melted butter
- 1/2 cup butter, softened
- 1 teaspoon vanilla extract

DIRECTIONS

1. Preheat oven to 350 degrees F (175 degrees C). Combine flour, baking powder, baking soda, cinnamon, nutmeg, ground cloves, and salt; set aside.
2. In a medium bowl, cream together the 1/2 cup of butter and white sugar. Add pumpkin, egg, and 1 teaspoon vanilla to butter mixture, and beat until creamy. Mix in dry ingredients. Drop on cookie sheet by tablespoonfuls; flatten slightly.
3. Bake for 15 to 20 minutes in the preheated oven. Cool cookies, then drizzle glaze with fork.
4. To Make Glaze: Combine confectioners' sugar, milk, 1 tablespoon melted butter, and 1 teaspoon vanilla. Add milk as needed, to achieve drizzling consistency.

PEANUT BUTTER CUP COOKIES

Servings: 40 | Prep: 25m | Cooks: 10m | Total: 1h35m | Additional: 1h

NUTRITION FACTS

Calories: 122 | Carbohydrates: 14.4g | Fat: 6.5g | Protein: 2.4g | Cholesterol: 11mg

INGREDIENTS

- 1 3/4 cups all-purpose flour
- 1/2 cup packed brown sugar
- 1/2 teaspoon salt
- 1 egg, beaten
- 1 teaspoon baking soda
- 1 teaspoon vanilla extract
- 1/2 cup butter, softened
- 2 tablespoons milk
- 1/2 cup white sugar
- 40 miniature chocolate covered peanut butter cups, unwrapped
- 1/2 cup peanut butter

DIRECTIONS

1. Preheat oven to 375 degrees F (190 degrees C). Sift together the flour, salt and baking soda; set aside.
2. Cream together the butter, sugar, peanut butter and brown sugar until fluffy. Beat in the egg, vanilla and milk. Add the flour mixture; mix well. Shape into 40 balls and place each into an ungreased mini muffin pan.
3. Bake at 375 degrees for about 8 minutes. Remove from oven and immediately press a mini peanut butter cup into each ball. Cool and carefully remove from pan.

SUGAR COOKIE ICING

Servings: 12 | Prep: 15m | Cooks: 0m | Total: 15m

NUTRITION FACTS

Calories: 43 | Carbohydrates: 10.9g | Fat: 0g | Protein: 0g | Cholesterol: <1mg

INGREDIENTS

- 1 cup confectioners' sugar
- 2 teaspoons light corn syrup
- 2 teaspoons milk
- 1/4 teaspoon almond extract

DIRECTIONS

1. In a small bowl, stir together confectioners' sugar and milk until smooth. Beat in corn syrup and almond extract until icing is smooth and glossy. If icing is too thick, add more corn syrup.
2. Divide into separate bowls, and add food colorings to each to desired intensity. Dip cookies, or paint them with a brush.

PEANUT BUTTER BARS

Servings: 12 | Prep: 25m | Cooks: 1h | Total: 1h25m | Additional: 1h

NUTRITION FACTS

Calories: 532 | Carbohydrates: 49.2g | Fat: 36.6g | Protein: 8.8g | Cholesterol: 41mg

INGREDIENTS

- 1 cup butter or margarine, melted
- 1 cup peanut butter
- 2 cups graham cracker crumbs
- 1 1/2 cups semisweet chocolate chips
- 2 cups confectioners' sugar
- 4 tablespoons peanut butter

DIRECTIONS

1. In a medium bowl, mix together the butter or margarine, graham cracker crumbs, confectioners' sugar, and 1 cup peanut butter until well blended. Press evenly into the bottom of an ungreased 9x13 inch pan.
2. In a metal bowl over simmering water, or in the microwave, melt the chocolate chips with the 4 tablespoons peanut butter, stirring occasionally until smooth. Spread over the prepared crust. Refrigerate for at least one hour before cutting into squares.

RASPBERRY AND ALMOND SHORTBREAD THUMBPRINTS

Servings: 36 | Prep: 30m | Cooks: 15m | Total: 1h15m | Additional: 27m

NUTRITION FACTS

Calories: 104 | Carbohydrates: 13.7g | Fat: 5.2g | Protein: 0.8g | Cholesterol: 14mg

INGREDIENTS

- 1 cup butter, softened
- 1/2 cup seedless raspberry jam
- 2/3 cup white sugar
- 1/2 cup confectioners' sugar
- 1/2 teaspoon almond extract
- 3/4 teaspoon almond extract
- 2 cups all-purpose flour
- 1 teaspoon milk

DIRECTIONS

1. Preheat oven to 350 degrees F (175 degrees C).
2. In a medium bowl, cream together butter and white sugar until smooth. Mix in 1/2 teaspoon almond extract. Mix in flour until dough comes together. Roll dough into 1 1/2 inch balls, and place on ungreased cookie sheets. Make a small hole in the center of each ball, using your thumb and finger, and fill the hole with preserves.
3. Bake for 14 to 18 minutes in preheated oven, or until lightly browned. Let cool 1 minute on the cookie sheet.
4. In a medium bowl, mix together the confectioners' sugar, 3/4 teaspoon almond extract, and milk until smooth. Drizzle lightly over warm cookies.

CHOCOLATE CRINKLES

Servings: 72 | Prep: 20m | Cooks: 12m | Total: 5h | Additional: 4h28m

NUTRITION FACTS

Calories: 58 | Carbohydrates: 9.8g | Fat: 2g | Protein: 0.9g | Cholesterol: 10mg

INGREDIENTS

- 1 cup unsweetened cocoa powder
- 2 cups all-purpose flour
- 2 cups white sugar
- 2 teaspoons baking powder
- 1/2 cup vegetable oil
- 1/2 teaspoon salt
- 4 eggs
- 1/2 cup confectioners' sugar
- 2 teaspoons vanilla extract

DIRECTIONS

1. In a medium bowl, mix together cocoa, white sugar, and vegetable oil. Beat in eggs one at a time, then stir in the vanilla. Combine the flour, baking powder, and salt; stir into the cocoa mixture. Cover dough, and chill for at least 4 hours.
2. Preheat oven to 350 degrees F (175 degrees C). Line cookie sheets with parchment paper. Roll dough into one inch balls. I like to use a number 50 size scoop. Coat each ball in confectioners' sugar before placing onto prepared cookie sheets.
3. Bake in preheated oven for 10 to 12 minutes. Let stand on the cookie sheet for a minute before transferring to wire racks to cool.

CRANBERRY PISTACHIO BISCOTTI

Servings: 36 | Prep: 25m | Cooks: 45m | Total: 1h20m | Additional: 10m

NUTRITION FACTS

Calories: 92 | Carbohydrates: 11.7g | Fat: 4.3g | Protein: 2.1g | Cholesterol: 10mg

INGREDIENTS

- 1/4 cup light olive oil
- 1 3/4 cups all-purpose flour
- 3/4 cup white sugar
- 1/4 teaspoon salt
- 2 teaspoons vanilla extract
- 1 teaspoon baking powder
- 1/2 teaspoon almond extract
- 1/2 cup dried cranberries
- 2 eggs
- 1 1/2 cups pistachio nuts

DIRECTIONS

1. Preheat the oven to 300 degrees F (150 degrees C).
2. In a large bowl, mix together oil and sugar until well blended. Mix in the vanilla and almond extracts, then beat in the eggs. Combine flour, salt, and baking powder; gradually stir into egg mixture. Mix in cranberries and nuts by hand.
3. Divide dough in half. Form two logs (12x2 inches) on a cookie sheet that has been lined with parchment paper. Dough may be sticky; wet hands with cool water to handle dough more easily.
4. Bake for 35 minutes in the preheated oven, or until logs are light brown. Remove from oven, and set aside to cool for 10 minutes. Reduce oven heat to 275 degrees F (135 degrees C).
5. Cut logs on diagonal into 3/4 inch thick slices. Lay on sides on parchment covered cookie sheet. Bake approximately 8 to 10 minutes, or until dry; cool.

SOFT CHRISTMAS COOKIES

Servings: 48 | Prep: 20m | Cooks: 8m | Total: 3h | Additional: 2h32m

NUTRITION FACTS

Calories: 97 | Carbohydrates: 13.8g | Fat: 4g | Protein: 1.3g | Cholesterol: 8mg

INGREDIENTS

- 3 3/4 cups all-purpose flour
- 1 1/2 cups white sugar

- 1 teaspoon baking powder
- 2 eggs
- 1/2 teaspoon salt
- 2 teaspoons vanilla extract
- 1 cup margarine, softened

DIRECTIONS

1. Sift flour, baking powder, and salt together, set aside. In a large bowl, cream together the margarine and sugar until light and fluffy. Beat in the eggs one at a time, then stir in the vanilla. Gradually blend in the sifted ingredients until fully absorbed. Cover dough, and chill for 2 hours.
2. Preheat oven to 400 degrees F (200 degrees C). Grease cookie sheets. On a clean floured surface, roll out small portions of chilled dough to 1/4 inch thickness. Cut out shapes using cookie cutters.
3. Bake 6 to 8 minutes in the preheated oven, or until edges are barely brown. Remove from cookie sheets to cool on wire racks.

COCONUT MACAROONS

Servings: 12 | Prep: 10m | Cooks: 25m | Total: 25m | Additional: 15m

NUTRITION FACTS

Calories: 287 | Carbohydrates: 40.7g | Fat: 12.4g | Protein: 4.4g | Cholesterol: 11mg

INGREDIENTS

- 2/3 cup all-purpose flour
- 1 (14 ounce) can sweetened condensed milk
- 5 1/2 cups flaked coconut
- 2 teaspoons vanilla extract
- 1/2 teaspoon salt

DIRECTIONS

1. Preheat oven to 350 degrees F (175 degrees C). Line cookie sheets with parchment paper or aluminum foil.
2. In a large bowl, stir together the flour, coconut and salt. Stir in the sweetened condensed milk and vanilla using your hands until well blended. Use an ice cream scoop to drop dough onto the prepared cookie sheets. Cookies should be about golf ball size.
3. Bake for 12 to 15 minutes in the preheated oven, until coconut is toasted.

MELT - IN - YOUR - MOUTH SHORTBREAD

Servings: 24 | Prep: 10m | Cooks: 15m | Total: 25m

NUTRITION FACTS

Calories: 111 | Carbohydrates: 9.7g | Fat: 7.8g | Protein: 0.9g | Cholesterol: 20mg

INGREDIENTS

- 1 cup butter, softened
- 1/4 cup cornstarch
- 1/2 cup confectioners' sugar
- 1 1/2 cups all-purpose flour

DIRECTIONS

1. Preheat the oven to 375 degrees F (190 degrees C).
2. Whip butter with an electric mixer until fluffy. Stir in the confectioners' sugar, cornstarch, and flour. Beat on low for one minute, then on high for 3 to 4 minutes. Drop cookies by spoonfuls 2 inches apart on an ungreased cookie sheet.
3. Bake for 12 to 15 minutes in the preheated oven. Watch that the edges don't brown too much. Cool on wire racks.

EILEEN'S SPICY GINGERBREAD MEN

Servings: 30 | Prep: 20m | Cooks: 10m | Total: 30m

NUTRITION FACTS

Calories: 88 | Carbohydrates: 14g | Fat: 3.3g | Protein: 1g | Cholesterol: 7mg

INGREDIENTS

- 1/2 cup margarine
- 1/2 teaspoon baking powder
- 1/2 cup sugar
- 1/2 teaspoon baking soda
- 1/2 cup molasses
- 1/2 teaspoon ground cinnamon
- 1 egg yolk
- 1 teaspoon ground cloves
- 2 cups sifted all-purpose flour
- 1 teaspoon ginger
- 1/2 teaspoon salt
- 1/2 teaspoon ground nutmeg

DIRECTIONS

1. In a large bowl, cream together the margarine and sugar until smooth. Stir in molasses and egg yolk. Combine the flour, salt, baking powder, baking soda, cinnamon, cloves, ginger, and nutmeg; blend into the molasses mixture until smooth. Cover, and chill for at least one hour.
2. Preheat the oven to 350 degrees F (175 degrees C). On a lightly floured surface, roll the dough out to 1/4 inch thickness. Cut into desired shapes with cookie cutters. Place cookies 2 inches apart on ungreased cookie sheets.
3. Bake for 8 to 10 minutes in the preheated oven, until firm. Remove from cookie sheets to cool on wire racks. Frost or decorate when cool.

RUSSIAN TEA CAKES

Servings: 36 | Prep: 20m | Cooks: 12m | Total: 35m | Additional: 3m

NUTRITION FACTS

Calories: 102 | Carbohydrates: 8.2g | Fat: 7.3g | Protein: 1.3g | Cholesterol: 14mg

INGREDIENTS

- 1 cup butter
- 2 cups all-purpose flour
- 1 teaspoon vanilla extract
- 1 cup chopped walnuts
- 6 tablespoons confectioners' sugar
- 1/3 cup confectioners' sugar for decoration

DIRECTIONS

1. Preheat oven to 350 degrees F (175 degrees C).
2. In a medium bowl, cream butter and vanilla until smooth. Combine the 6 tablespoons confectioners' sugar and flour; stir into the butter mixture until just blended. Mix in the chopped walnuts. Roll dough into 1 inch balls, and place them 2 inches apart on an ungreased cookie sheet.
3. Bake for 12 minutes in the preheated oven. When cool, roll in remaining confectioners' sugar. I also like to roll mine in the sugar a second time.

WHITE CHOCOLATE AND CRANBERRY COOKIES

Servings: 24 | Prep: 15m | Cooks: 10m | Total: 50m | Additional: 25m

NUTRITION FACTS

Calories: 147 | Carbohydrates: 21.9g | Fat: 6.1g | Protein: 1.5g | Cholesterol: 19mg

INGREDIENTS

- 1/2 cup butter, softened

- 1 1/2 cups all-purpose flour
- 1/2 cup packed brown sugar
- 1/2 teaspoon baking soda
- 1/2 cup white sugar
- 3/4 cup white chocolate chips
- 1 egg
- 1 cup dried cranberries
- 1 tablespoon brandy

DIRECTIONS

1. Preheat oven to 375 degrees F (190 degrees C). Grease cookie sheets.
2. In a large bowl, cream together the butter, brown sugar, and white sugar until smooth. Beat in the egg and brandy. Combine the flour and baking soda; stir into the sugar mixture. Mix in the white chocolate chips and cranberries. Drop by heaping spoonfuls onto prepared cookie sheets.
3. Bake for 8 to 10 minutes in the preheated oven. For best results, take them out while they are still doughy. Allow cookies to cool for 1 minute on the cookie sheets before transferring to wire racks to cool completely.

CRANBERRY ORANGE COOKIES

Servings: 48 | Prep: 20m | Cooks: 14m | Total: 34m

NUTRITION FACTS

Calories: 110 | Carbohydrates: 16.2g | Fat: 4.8g | Protein: 1.1g | Cholesterol: 14mg

INGREDIENTS

- 1 cup butter, softened
- 1/2 teaspoon baking soda
- 1 cup white sugar
- 1/2 teaspoon salt
- 1/2 cup packed brown sugar
- 2 cups chopped cranberries
- 1 egg
- 1/2 cup chopped walnuts (optional)
- 1 teaspoon grated orange zest
- 1/2 teaspoon grated orange zest
- 2 tablespoons orange juice
- 3 tablespoons orange juice
- 2 1/2 cups all-purpose flour
- 1 1/2 cups confectioners' sugar

DIRECTIONS

1. Preheat the oven to 375 degrees F (190 degrees C).
2. In a large bowl, cream together the butter, white sugar and brown sugar until smooth. Beat in the egg until well blended. Mix in 1 teaspoon orange zest and 2 tablespoons orange juice. Combine the flour, baking soda and salt; stir into the orange mixture. Mix in cranberries and if using, walnuts, until evenly distributed. Drop dough by rounded tablespoonfuls onto ungreased cookie sheets. Cookies should be spaced at least 2 inches apart.
3. Bake for 12 to 14 minutes in the preheated oven, until the edges are golden. Remove from cookie sheets to cool on wire racks.
4. In a small bowl, mix together 1/2 teaspoon orange zest, 3 tablespoons orange juice and confectioners' sugar until smooth. Spread over the tops of cooled cookies. Let stand until set.

JAM FILLED BUTTER COOKIES

Servings: 36 | Prep: 30m | Cooks: 10m | Total: 40m

NUTRITION FACTS

Calories: 82 | Carbohydrates: 10.5g | Fat: 4.1g | Protein: 0.8g | Cholesterol: 22mg

INGREDIENTS

- 3/4 cup butter, softened
- 1 3/4 cups all-purpose flour
- 1/2 cup white sugar
- 1/2 cup fruit preserves, any flavor
- 2 egg yolks

DIRECTIONS

1. Preheat the oven to 375 degrees F (190 degrees C).
2. In a medium bowl, cream together the butter, white sugar and egg yolks. Mix in flour a little bit at a time until a soft dough forms. Roll dough into 1 inch balls. If dough is too soft, refrigerate for 15 to 20 minutes. Place balls 2 inches apart onto ungreased cookie sheets. Use your finger or an instrument of similar size to make a well in the center of each cookie. Fill the hole with 1/2 teaspoon of preserves.
3. Bake for 8 to 10 minutes in the preheated oven, until golden brown on the bottom. Remove from cookie sheets to cool on wire racks.

MOLASSES SUGAR COOKIES

Servings: 72 | Prep: 25m | Cooks: 15m | Total: 3h40m | Additional: 3h

NUTRITION FACTS

Calories: 93 | Carbohydrates: 12.7g | Fat: 4.5g | Protein: 0.9g | Cholesterol: 5mg

INGREDIENTS

- 1 1/2 cups shortening
- 4 teaspoons baking soda
- 2 cups white sugar
- 2 teaspoons ground cinnamon
- 1/2 cup molasses
- 1 teaspoon ground cloves
- 2 eggs
- 1 teaspoon ground ginger
- 4 cups all-purpose flour
- 1 teaspoon salt

DIRECTIONS

1. Melt the shortening in a large pan on the stove, and cool.
2. Add sugar, eggs, and molasses, beat well.
3. In a separate bowl, sift dry ingredients together and add to the pan. Mix well and chill 3 hours or overnight.
4. Form into walnut-size balls. Roll in granulated sugar. Place on greased cookie sheet about 2 inches apart.
5. Bake at 375 degrees F (190 degrees C) for 8-10 minutes.
6. Store in an airtight container to keep from getting overly crisp. If they do lose their softness, an easy way to restore it is to place one slice of fresh bread in the container with the cookies for a couple of hours or overnight and they will be soft again.

BISCOTTI

Servings: 42 | Prep: 15m | Cooks: 25m | Total: 40m

NUTRITION FACTS

Calories: 83 | Carbohydrates: 12.3g | Fat: 3.1g | Protein: 1.4g | Cholesterol: 13mg

INGREDIENTS

- 1/2 cup vegetable oil
- 3 eggs
- 1 cup white sugar
- 1 tablespoon baking powder
- 3 1/4 cups all-purpose flour
- 1 tablespoon anise extract, or 3 drops anise oil

DIRECTIONS

1. Preheat the oven to 375 degrees F (190 degrees C). Grease cookie sheets or line with parchment paper.
2. In a medium bowl, beat together the oil, eggs, sugar and anise flavoring until well blended. Combine the flour and baking powder, stir into the egg mixture to form a heavy dough. Divide dough into two pieces. Form each piece into a roll as long as your cookie sheet. Place roll onto the prepared cookie sheet, and press down to 1/2 inch thickness.
3. Bake for 25 to 30 minutes in the preheated oven, until golden brown. Remove from the baking sheet to cool on a wire rack. When The cookies are cool enough to handle, slice each one crosswise into 1/2 inch slices. Place the slices cut side up back onto the baking sheet. Bake for an additional 6 to 10 minutes on each side. Slices should be lightly toasted.

CREAM CHEESE SUGAR COOKIES

Servings: 72 | Prep: 15m | Cooks: 10m | Total: 9h25m | Additional: 9h

NUTRITION FACTS

Calories: 53 | Carbohydrates: 5.8g | Fat: 3.1g | Protein: 0.6g | Cholesterol: 11mg

INGREDIENTS

- 1 cup white sugar
- 1/2 teaspoon almond extract
- 1 cup butter, softened
- 1/2 teaspoon vanilla extract
- 1 (3 ounce) package cream cheese, softened
- 1 egg yolk
- 1/2 teaspoon salt
- 2 1/4 cups all-purpose flour

DIRECTIONS

1. In a large bowl, combine the sugar, butter, cream cheese, salt, almond and vanilla extracts, and egg yolk. Beat until smooth. Stir in flour until well blended. Chill the dough for 8 hours, or overnight.
2. Preheat oven to 375 degrees F (190 degrees C).
3. On a lightly floured surface, roll out the dough 1/3 at a time to 1/8 inch thickness, refrigerating remaining dough until ready to use. Cut into desired shapes with lightly floured cookie cutters. Place 1 inch apart on ungreased cookie sheets. Leave cookies plain for frosting, or brush with slightly beaten egg white and sprinkle with candy sprinkles or colored sugar.
4. Bake for 7 to 10 minutes in the preheated oven, or until light and golden brown. Cool cookies completely before frosting.

MOLASSES COOKIES

Servings: 30 | Prep: 10m | Cooks: 10m | Total: 1h20m | Additional: 1h

NUTRITION FACTS

Calories: 120 | Carbohydrates: 18.6g | Fat: 4.7g | Protein: 1.1g | Cholesterol: 6mg

INGREDIENTS

- 3/4 cup margarine, melted
- 1/2 teaspoon salt
- 1 cup white sugar
- 1 teaspoon ground cinnamon
- 1 egg
- 1/2 teaspoon ground cloves
- 1/4 cup molasses
- 1/2 teaspoon ground ginger
- 2 cups all-purpose flour
- 1/2 cup white sugar
- 2 teaspoons baking soda

DIRECTIONS

1. In a medium bowl, mix together the melted margarine, 1 cup sugar, and egg until smooth. Stir in the molasses. Combine the flour, baking soda, salt, cinnamon, cloves, and ginger; blend into the molasses mixture. Cover, and chill dough for 1 hour.
2. Preheat oven to 375 degrees F (190 degrees C). Roll dough into walnut sized balls, and roll them in the remaining white sugar. Place cookies 2 inches apart onto ungreased baking sheets.
3. Bake for 8 to 10 minutes in the preheated oven, until tops are cracked. Cool on wire racks.

GINGERBREAD MEN

Servings: 30 | Prep: 25m | Cooks: 12m | Total: 1h37m | Additional: 1h

NUTRITION FACTS

Calories: 79 | Carbohydrates: 11.5g | Fat: 3.3g | Protein: 1g | Cholesterol: 14mg

INGREDIENTS

- 1 (3.5 ounce) package cook and serve butterscotch pudding mix
- 1 1/2 cups all-purpose flour
- 1/2 cup butter
- 1/2 teaspoon baking soda
- 1/2 cup packed brown sugar

- 1 1/2 teaspoons ground ginger
- 1 egg
- 1 teaspoon ground cinnamon

DIRECTIONS

1. In a medium bowl, cream together the dry butterscotch pudding mix, butter, and brown sugar until smooth. Stir in the egg. Combine the flour, baking soda, ginger, and cinnamon; stir into the pudding mixture. Cover, and chill dough until firm, about 1 hour.
2. Preheat the oven to 350 degrees F (175 degrees C). Grease baking sheets. On a floured board, roll dough out to about 1/8 inch thickness, and cut into man shapes using a cookie cutter. Place cookies 2 inches apart on the prepared baking sheets.
3. Bake for 10 to 12 minutes in the preheated oven, until cookies are golden at the edges. Cool on wire racks.

BUCKEYE BALLS

Servings: 30 | Prep: 45m | Cooks: 10m | Total: 1h25m | Additional: 30m

NUTRITION FACTS

Calories: 204 | Carbohydrates: 22.8g | Fat: 12g | Protein: 3.7g | Cholesterol: 8mg

INGREDIENTS

- 1 1/2 cups creamy peanut butter
- 4 cups sifted confectioners' sugar
- 1/2 cup butter, softened
- 6 ounces semi-sweet chocolate chips
- 1 teaspoon vanilla extract
- 2 tablespoons shortening

DIRECTIONS

1. Line a baking sheet with waxed paper; set aside.
2. In a medium bowl, mix peanut butter, butter, vanilla, and confectioners' sugar with hands to form a smooth stiff dough. Shape into balls using 2 teaspoons of dough for each ball. Place on prepared pan, and refrigerate.
3. Melt shortening and chocolate together in a metal bowl over a pan of lightly simmering water. Stir occasionally until smooth, and remove from heat.
4. Remove balls from refrigerator. Insert a wooden toothpick into a ball, and dip into melted chocolate. Return to wax paper, chocolate side down, and remove toothpick. Repeat with remaining balls. Refrigerate for 30 minutes to set.

CARAMEL SHORTBREAD SQUARES

Servings: 40 | Prep: 10m | Cooks: 25m | Total: 35m

NUTRITION FACTS

Calories: 119 | Carbohydrates: 13.2g | Fat: 7.3g | Protein: 1.1g | Cholesterol: 17mg

INGREDIENTS

- 2/3 cup butter, softened
- 1/2 cup packed light brown sugar
- 1/4 cup white sugar
- 2 tablespoons light corn syrup
- 1 1/3 cups all-purpose flour
- 1/2 cup sweetened condensed milk
- 1/2 cup butter
- 1 1/4 cups milk chocolate chips

DIRECTIONS

1. Preheat oven to 350 degrees F (175 C).
2. In a medium bowl, mix together 2/3 cup butter, white sugar, and flour until evenly crumbly. Press into a 9 inch square baking pan. Bake for 20 minutes.
3. In a 2 quart saucepan, combine 1/2 cup butter, brown sugar, corn syrup, and sweetened condensed milk. Bring to a boil. Continue to boil for 5 minutes. Remove from heat and beat vigorously with a wooden spoon for about 3 minutes. Pour over baked crust (warm or cool). Cool until it begins to firm.
4. Place chocolate in a microwave-safe bowl. Heat for 1 minute, then stir and continue to heat and stir at 20 second intervals until chocolate is melted and smooth. Pour chocolate over the caramel layer and spread evenly to cover completely. Chill. Cut into 1 inch squares. These need to be small because they are so rich.

CARAMEL FILLED CHOCOLATE COOKIES

Servings: 24 | Prep: 20m | Cooks: 10m | Total: 3h | Additional: 2h30m

NUTRITION FACTS

Calories: 253 | Carbohydrates: 33.1g | Fat: 13g | Protein: 3.4g | Cholesterol: 37mg

INGREDIENTS

- 1 cup butter, softened
- 1 teaspoon baking soda
- 1 cup white sugar

- 3/4 cup unsweetened cocoa powder
- 1 cup packed brown sugar
- 1 cup chopped walnuts
- 2 eggs
- 1 tablespoon white sugar
- 2 teaspoons vanilla extract
- 48 chocolate-covered caramel candies
- 2 1/4 cups all-purpose flour

DIRECTIONS

1. Beat butter until creamy. Gradually beat in white sugar and brown sugar. Beat in eggs and vanilla. Combine flour, baking soda, and cocoa. Gradually add to butter mixture, beating well. Stir in 1/2 cup walnuts. Cover and chill at least 2 hours.
2. Preheat oven to 375 degrees F (190 degrees C).
3. Combine remaining 1/2 cup nuts with the 1 tablespoon sugar. Divide the dough into 4 parts. Work with one part at a time, leaving the remainder in the refrigerator until needed. Divide each part into 12 pieces. Quickly press each piece of dough around a chocolate covered caramel. Roll into a ball. Dip the tops into the sugar mixture. Place sugar side up, 2 inches apart on greased baking sheets.
4. Bake for 8 minutes in the preheated oven. Let cool for 3 to 4 minutes on the baking sheets before removing to wire racks to cool completely.

CRANBERRY HOOTYCREEKS

Servings: 18 | Prep: 25m | Cooks: 0m | Total: 25m

NUTRITION FACTS

Calories: 126 | Carbohydrates: 21.2g | Fat: 4.2g | Protein: 1.7g | Cholesterol: 1mg

INGREDIENTS

- 5/8 cup all-purpose flour
- 1/3 cup packed brown sugar
- 1/2 cup rolled oats
- 1/3 cup white sugar
- 1/2 cup all-purpose flour
- 1/2 cup dried cranberries
- 1/2 teaspoon baking soda
- 1/2 cup white chocolate chips
- 1/2 teaspoon salt
- 1/2 cup chopped pecans

DIRECTIONS

1. Layer the ingredients in a 1 quart or 1 liter jar, in the order listed.
2. Attach a tag with the following instructions: Cranberry Hootycreeks 1. Preheat oven to 350 degrees F (175 degrees C). Grease a cookie sheet or line with parchment paper. 2. In a medium bowl, beat together 1/2 cup softened butter, 1 egg and 1 teaspoon of vanilla until fluffy. Add the entire jar of ingredients, and mix together by hand until well blended. Drop by heaping spoonfuls onto the prepared baking sheets. 3. Bake for 8 to 10 minutes, or until edges start to brown. Cool on baking sheets, or remove to cool on wire racks.

WHITE CHOCOLATE MACADAMIA NUT COOKIES
Servings: 24 | Prep: 15m | Cooks: 8m | Total: 23m

NUTRITION FACTS

Calories: 193 | Carbohydrates: 17.6g | Fat: 13.2g | Protein: 2.2g | Cholesterol: 20mg

INGREDIENTS

- 1/2 cup butter
- 1/2 teaspoon baking soda
- 3/4 cup white sugar
- 1/2 teaspoon salt
- 1 egg
- 8 ounces white chocolate, chopped
- 1 teaspoon vanilla extract
- 1 (6.5 ounce) jar macadamia nuts, chopped
- 11/4 cups all-purpose flour

DIRECTIONS

1. Preheat oven to 375 degrees F (190 degrees C).
2. In a medium bowl, cream together the butter and sugar. Stir in the egg and vanilla. Combine the flour, baking soda and salt, stir into the creamed mixture. Finally, stir in the white chocolate and nuts. Drop cookies by heaping teaspoonfuls onto an ungreased cookie sheet, about 2 inches apart.
3. Bake for 8 to 10 minutes in the preheated oven, until lightly browned. Cool on wire racks. When cool, store in an airtight container.

PEPPERMINT MERINGUES
Servings: 48 | Prep: 20m | Cooks: 1h30m | Total: 5h | Additional: 3h10m

NUTRITION FACTS

Calories: 13 | Carbohydrates: 3.2g | Fat: 0g | Protein: 0.2g | Cholesterol: 0mg

INGREDIENTS

- 2 egg whites
- 1/2 cup white sugar
- 1/8 teaspoon salt
- 2 peppermint candy canes, crushed
- 1/8 teaspoon cream of tartar

DIRECTIONS

1. Preheat oven to 225 degrees F (110 degrees C). Line 2 cookie sheets with foil.
2. In a large glass or metal mixing bowl, beat egg whites, salt, and cream of tartar to soft peaks. Gradually add sugar, continuing to beat until whites form stiff peaks. Drop by spoonfuls 1 inch apart on the prepared cookie sheets. Sprinkle crushed peppermint candy over the cookies.
3. Bake for 1 1/2 hours in preheated oven. Meringues should be completely dry on the inside. Do not allow them to brown. Turn off oven. Keep oven door ajar, and let meringues sit in the oven until completely cool. Loosen from foil with metal spatula. Store loosely covered in cool dry place for up to 2 months.

PEANUT BLOSSOMS

Servings: 84 | Prep: 30m | Cooks: 12m | Total: 1h30m | Additional: 48m

NUTRITION FACTS

Calories: 116 | Carbohydrates: 14.3g | Fat: 6g | Protein: 1.9g | Cholesterol: 6mg

INGREDIENTS

- 1 cup shortening
- 2 teaspoons vanilla extract
- 1 cup peanut butter
- 3 1/2 cups all-purpose flour
- 1 cup packed brown sugar
- 2 teaspoons baking soda
- 1 cup white sugar
- 1 teaspoon salt
- 2 eggs
- 1/2 cup white sugar for decoration
- 1/4 cup milk
- 2 (9 ounce) bags milk chocolate candy kisses, unwrapped

DIRECTIONS

1. Preheat oven to 375 degrees F (190 degrees C). Grease cookie sheets.

2. In a large bowl, cream together the shortening, peanut butter, brown sugar, and 1 cup white sugar until smooth. Beat in the eggs one at a time, and stir in the milk and vanilla. Combine the flour, baking soda, and salt; stir into the peanut butter mixture until well blended. Shape tablespoonfuls of dough into balls, and roll in remaining white sugar. Place cookies 2 inches apart on the prepared cookie sheets.

3. Bake for 10 to12 minutes in the preheated oven. Remove from oven, and immediately press a chocolate kiss into each cookie. Allow to cool completely; the kiss will harden as it cools.

BROWNIE BISCOTTI

Servings: 30 | Prep: 30m | Cooks: 45m | Total: 1h55m | Additional: 40m

NUTRITION FACTS

Calories: 91 | Carbohydrates: 12.6g | Fat: 4.2g | Protein: 1.7g | Cholesterol: 25mg

INGREDIENTS

- 1/3 cup butter, softened
- 2 teaspoons baking powder
- 2/3 cup white sugar
- 1/2 cup miniature semisweet chocolate chips
- 2 eggs
- 1/4 cup chopped walnuts
- 1 teaspoon vanilla extract
- 1 egg yolk, beaten
- 1 3/4 cups all-purpose flour
- 1 tablespoon water
- 1/3 cup unsweetened cocoa powder

DIRECTIONS

1. Preheat oven to 375 degrees F (190 degrees C). Grease baking sheets, or line with parchment paper.

2. In a large bowl, cream together the butter and sugar until smooth. Beat in the eggs one at a time, then stir in the vanilla. Combine the flour, cocoa and baking powder; stir into the creamed mixture until well blended. Dough will be stiff, so mix in the last bit by hand. Mix in the chocolate chips and walnuts.

3. Divide dough into two equal parts. Shape into 9x2x1 inch loaves. Place onto baking sheet 4 inches apart. Brush with mixture of water and yolk.

4. Bake for 20 to 25 minutes in the preheated oven, or until firm. Cool on baking sheet for 30 minutes.

5. Using a serrated knife, slice the loaves diagonally into 1 inch slices. Return the slices to the baking sheet, placing them on their sides. Bake for 10 to 15 minutes on each side, or until dry. Cool completely and store in an airtight container.

WHIPPED SHORTBREAD COOKIES

Servings: 36 | Prep: 15m | Cooks: 20m | Total: 35m

NUTRITION FACTS

Calories: 75 | Carbohydrates: 6.8g | Fat: 5.2g | Protein: 0.6g | Cholesterol: 14mg

INGREDIENTS

- 1 cup butter, softened
- 1/4 cup red maraschino cherries, quartered
- 1 1/2 cups all-purpose flour
- 1/4 cup green maraschino cherries, quartered
- 1/2 cup confectioners' sugar

DIRECTIONS

1. Preheat oven to 350 degrees F (175 degrees C).
2. In a large bowl, combine butter, flour, and confectioners' sugar. With an electric mixer, beat for 10 minutes, until light and fluffy. Spoon onto cookie sheets, spacing cookies 2 inches apart. Place a piece of maraschino cherry onto the middle of each cookie, alternating between red and green.
3. Bake for 15 to 17 minutes in the preheated oven, or until the bottoms of the cookies are lightly browned. Remove from oven, and let cool on cookie sheet for 5 minutes, then transfer cookies on to wire rack to cool. Store in an airtight container, separating each layer with waxed paper.

ROSENMUNNAR

Servings: 36 | Prep: 40m | Cooks: 15m | Total: 55m

NUTRITION FACTS

Calories: 93 | Carbohydrates: 11.1g | Fat: 5.2g | Protein: 0.8g | Cholesterol: 14mg

INGREDIENTS

- 1 cup butter, softened
- 1/2 cup white sugar
- 2 cups sifted all-purpose flour
- 1/2 cup any flavor fruit jam

DIRECTIONS

1. Preheat oven to 375 degrees F (190 degrees C).
2. Cream butter and sugar until light and fluffy. Add sifted flour, and mix well. Shape dough into 1-inch balls and place on cookie sheets. Imprint your thumb in the center to make a 1/2-inch indentation. Fill with your favorite preserves.

3. Bake 15 to 20 minutes or until golden brown at the edges.

SNOWBALLS

Servings: 30 | Prep: 30m | Cooks: 15m | Total: 45m

NUTRITION FACTS

Calories: 135 | Carbohydrates: 13g | Fat: 8.8g | Protein: 1.4g | Cholesterol: 16mg

INGREDIENTS

- 1 cup butter
- 2 1/4 cups all-purpose flour
- 1/2 cup confectioners' sugar
- 1 cup chopped pecans
- 1/4 teaspoon salt
- 1/3 cup confectioners' sugar for dusting, or as needed
- 1 teaspoon vanilla extract
- 1/4 cup finely crushed peppermint candy canes (optional)

DIRECTIONS

1. Preheat oven to 350 degrees F (175 degrees C).
2. Cream the butter with 1/2 cup of the confectioners' sugar and the vanilla. Mix in the flour, pecans, and salt. Roll about 1 tablespoon or so of dough into balls and place on an ungreased cookie sheet.
3. Bake in preheated oven until bottoms are golden, about 15 minutes. Do not allow these cookies to get too brown: it's better to undercook them than to overcook them. While cookies are still hot, roll them in confectioners' sugar. Once they have cooled, roll them in confectioners' sugar once more.

CHOCOLATE RUM BALLS

Servings: 48 | Prep: 45m | Cooks: 0m | Total: 45m

NUTRITION FACTS

Calories: 99 | Carbohydrates: 12.3g | Fat: 4.8g | Protein: 1.2g | Cholesterol: 0mg

INGREDIENTS

- 3 1/4 cups crushed vanilla wafers
- 1 1/2 cups chopped walnuts
- 3/4 cup confectioners' sugar
- 3 tablespoons light corn syrup
- 1/4 cup unsweetened cocoa powder

- 1/2 cup rum

DIRECTIONS

1. In a large bowl, stir together the crushed vanilla wafers, 3/4 cup confectioners' sugar, cocoa, and nuts. Blend in corn syrup and rum.
2. Shape into 1 inch balls, and roll in additional confectioners' sugar. Store in an airtight container for several days to develop the flavor. Roll again in confectioners' sugar before serving.

MCCORMICK GINGERBREAD MEN COOKIES

Servings: 24 | Prep: 20m | Cooks: 10m | Total: 4h30m

NUTRITION FACTS

Calories: 158 | Carbohydrates: 24g | Fat: 6.1g | Protein: 2g | Cholesterol: 23mg

INGREDIENTS

- 3 cups flour
- 3/4 cup butter, softened
- 2 teaspoons McCormick Ground Ginger
- 3/4 cup firmly packed brown sugar
- 1 teaspoon McCormick Ground Cinnamon
- 1/2 cup molasses
- 1 teaspoon baking soda
- 1 egg
- 1/4 teaspoon McCormick Ground Nutmeg
- 1 teaspoon McCormick Pure Vanilla Extract
- 1/4 teaspoon salt

DIRECTIONS

1. Mix flour, ginger, cinnamon, baking soda, nutmeg and salt in large bowl. Beat butter and brown sugar in another large bowl with electric mixer on medium speed until light and fluffy. Add molasses, egg and vanilla; beat well. Gradually beat in flour mixture on low speed until well mixed. Press dough into a thick flat disk. Wrap in plastic wrap. Refrigerate 4 hours or overnight.
2. Preheat oven to 350 degrees F. Roll out dough to 1/4-inch thickness on lightly floured work surface. Cut into gingerbread men shapes with 5-inch cookie cutter. Place 1 inch apart on ungreased baking sheets.
3. Bake 8 to 10 minutes or until edges of cookies are set and just begin to brown. Cool on baking sheets 1 to 2 minutes. Remove to wire racks; cool completely. Decorate cooled cookies as desired. Store cookies in airtight container up to 5 days.

BUTTER SNOW FLAKES

Servings: 36 | Prep: 15m | Cooks: 15m | Total: 1h | Additional: 30m

NUTRITION FACTS

Calories: 105 | Carbohydrates: 11.6g | Fat: 6.1g | Protein: 1.1g | Cholesterol: 22mg

INGREDIENTS

- 2 1/4 cups all-purpose flour
- 1 cup white sugar
- 1/4 teaspoon salt
- 1 egg yolk
- 1/4 teaspoon ground cinnamon
- 1 teaspoon vanilla extract
- 1 cup butter
- 1 teaspoon orange zest
- 1 (3 ounce) package cream cheese, softened

DIRECTIONS

1. Preheat oven to 350 degrees F (175 degrees C). Sift together the flour, salt, and cinnamon; set aside.
2. In a medium bowl, cream together butter and cream cheese. Add sugar and egg yolk; beat until light and fluffy. Stir in the vanilla and orange zest. Gradually blend in the dry ingredients. Fill a cookie press or pastry bag with dough, and form cookies on an ungreased cookie sheet.
3. Bake for 12 to 15 minutes in the preheated oven, or until the cookies are golden brown on the peaks and on the bottoms. Remove from cookie sheets at once to cool on wire racks.

CHEWY CHOCOLATE COOKIES

Servings: 48 | Prep: 15m | Cooks: 10m | Total: 55m | Additional: 30m

NUTRITION FACTS

Calories: 134 | Carbohydrates: 17.5g | Fat: 7.3g | Protein: 1.4g | Cholesterol: 20mg

INGREDIENTS

- 1 1/4 cups butter, softened
- 3/4 cup unsweetened cocoa powder
- 2 cups white sugar
- 1 teaspoon baking soda
- 2 eggs
- 1/2 teaspoon salt
- 2 teaspoons vanilla extract

- 2 cups semisweet chocolate chips
- 2 cups all-purpose flour

DIRECTIONS

1. Preheat oven to 350 degrees F (175 degrees C).
2. In a large bowl, cream together the butter and sugar until light and fluffy. Beat in the eggs one at a time, then stir in the vanilla. Sift together the flour, cocoa, baking soda, and salt; stir into the creamed mixture. Mix in the chocolate chips. Drop dough by teaspoonfuls onto ungreased cookie sheets.
3. Bake 8 to 9 minutes in the preheated oven. Cookies will be soft. Cool slightly on cookie sheet; remove from sheet onto wire rack to cool completely.

GRANDMA'S GINGERSNAPS

Servings: 36 | Prep: 15m | Cooks: 10m | Total: 30m | Additional: 5m

NUTRITION FACTS

Calories: 100 | Carbohydrates: 15.5g | Fat: 4g | Protein: 1g | Cholesterol: 5mg

INGREDIENTS

- 3/4 cup margarine
- 1 tablespoon ground ginger
- 1 cup white sugar
- 1 teaspoon ground cinnamon
- 1 egg
- 2 teaspoons baking soda
- 1/4 cup molasses
- 1/2 teaspoon salt
- 2 cups all-purpose flour
- 1/2 cup white sugar for decoration

DIRECTIONS

1. Preheat oven to 350 degrees F (175 degrees C).
2. In a medium bowl, cream together the margarine and 1 cup white sugar until smooth. Beat in the egg and molasses until well blended. Combine the flour, ginger, cinnamon, baking soda and salt; stir into the molasses mixture to form a dough. Roll dough into 1 inch balls and roll the balls in the remaining sugar. Place cookies 2 inches apart onto ungreased cookie sheets.
3. Bake for 8 to 10 minutes in the preheated oven. Allow cookies to cool on baking sheet for 5 minutes before removing to a wire rack to cool completely.

ORIGINAL NESTLE TOLL HOUSE CHOCOLATE CHIP COOKIES

Servings: 30 | Prep: 15m | Cooks: 9m | Total: 39m

NUTRITION FACTS

Calories: 108 | Carbohydrates: 12.7g | Fat: 6.2g | Protein: 1.4g | Cholesterol: 14mg

INGREDIENTS

- 2 1/4 cups all-purpose flour
- 3/4 cup packed brown sugar
- 1 teaspoon baking soda
- 1 teaspoon vanilla extract
- 1 teaspoon salt
- 2 large eggs
- 1 cup butter, softened
- 2 cups NESTLE TOLL HOUSE Semi-Sweet Chocolate Morsels
- 3/4 cup granulated sugar
- 1 cup chopped nuts

DIRECTIONS

1. Preheat oven to 375 degrees F.
2. Combine flour, baking soda and salt in small bowl. Beat butter, granulated sugar, brown sugar and vanilla extract in large mixer bowl until creamy. Add eggs, one at a time, beating well after each addition. Gradually beat in flour mixture. Stir in morsels and nuts. Drop by rounded tablespoon onto ungreased baking sheets.
3. Bake for 9 to 11 minutes or until golden brown. Cool on baking sheets for 2 minutes; remove to wire racks to cool completely.

CHEESECAKE TOPPED BROWNIES

Servings: 40 | Prep: 20m | Cooks: 45m | Total: 1h5m

NUTRITION FACTS

Calories: 170 | Carbohydrates: 24.4g | Fat: 7.7g | Protein: 2.1g | Cholesterol: 16mg

INGREDIENTS

- 1 (21.5 ounce) package brownie mix
- 1 (14 ounce) can sweetened condensed milk
- 1 (8 ounce) package cream cheese, softened
- 1 egg

- 2 tablespoons butter, softened
- 1 teaspoon vanilla extract
- 1 tablespoon cornstarch
- 1 (16 ounce) container prepared chocolate frosting

DIRECTIONS

1. Preheat oven 350 degrees F (175 degrees C). Grease a 9x13 inch baking pan.
2. Prepare brownie mix according to the directions on the package. Spread into prepared baking pan.
3. In a medium bowl, beat cream cheese, butter and cornstarch until fluffy. Gradually beat in sweetened condensed milk, egg and vanilla until smooth. Pour cream cheese mixture evenly over brownie batter.
4. Bake in preheated oven for 45 minutes, or until top is lightly browned. Allow to cool, spread with frosting, and cut into bars. Store covered in refrigerator, or freeze in a single layer for up to 2 weeks.

GRAMMA'S DATE SQUARES

Servings: 12 | Prep: 25m | Cooks: 25m | Total: 50m

NUTRITION FACTS

Calories: 363 | Carbohydrates: 63.7g | Fat: 12.5g | Protein: 3.7g | Cholesterol: 31mg

INGREDIENTS

- 1 1/2 cups rolled oats
- 3/4 cup butter, softened
- 1 1/2 cups sifted pastry flour
- 3/4 pound pitted dates, diced
- 1/4 teaspoon salt
- 1 cup water
- 3/4 teaspoon baking soda
- 1/3 cup packed brown sugar
- 1 cup packed brown sugar
- 1 teaspoon lemon juice

DIRECTIONS

1. Preheat oven to 350 degrees F (175 degrees C).
2. In a large bowl, combine oats, pastry flour, salt, 1 cup brown sugar, and baking soda. Mix in the butter until crumbly. Press half of the mixture into the bottom of a 9 inch square baking pan.
3. In a small saucepan over medium heat, combine the dates, water, and 1/3 cup brown sugar. Bring to a boil, and cook until thickened. Stir in lemon juice, and remove from heat. Spread the filling over the base, and pat the remaining crumb mixture on top.

4. Bake for 20 to 25 minutes in preheated oven, or until top is lightly toasted. Cool before cutting into squares.

BUTTER RICH SPRITZ BUTTER COOKIES

Servings: 36 | Prep: 10m | Cooks: 6m | Total: 18m | Additional: 2m

NUTRITION FACTS

Calories: 96 | Carbohydrates: 10.8g | Fat: 5.4g | Protein: 1.1g | Cholesterol: 25mg

INGREDIENTS

- 2 1/2 cups all-purpose flour
- 2 egg yolks
- 1/2 teaspoon salt
- 1/2 teaspoon almond extract
- 1 cup butter, softened
- 1 teaspoon vanilla extract
- 1 1/4 cups confectioners' sugar

DIRECTIONS

1. Preheat the oven to 400 degrees F (200 degrees C). Sift together the flour and salt; set aside.
2. In a medium bowl, cream together the butter and sugar. Stir in the egg yolks, almond extract and vanilla extract. Gradually blend in the sifted ingredients. Fill a cookie press with dough and shoot cookies about 1 1/2 inches apart onto an ungreased cookie sheet. If you like, decorate with sugar or sprinkles at this time.
3. Bake for 6 to 8 minutes in the preheated oven.

GINGERBREAD BOYS

Servings: 60 | Prep: 15m | Cooks: 10m | Total: 2h25m | Additional: 2h

NUTRITION FACTS

Calories: 73 | Carbohydrates: 10.4g | Fat: 3.2g | Protein: 0.8g | Cholesterol: 11mg

INGREDIENTS

- 1 cup butter, softened
- 2 teaspoons baking soda
- 1 1/2 cups white sugar
- 2 teaspoons ground cinnamon
- 1 egg

* 1 teaspoon ground ginger
* 1 1/2 tablespoons orange zest
* 1/2 teaspoon ground cloves
* 2 tablespoons dark corn syrup
* 1/2 teaspoon salt
* 3 cups all-purpose flour

DIRECTIONS

1. Cream the butter and the sugar together. Add the egg and mix well. Mix in the orange peel and dark corn syrup. Add the flour, baking soda, cinnamon, ginger, ground cloves and salt, mixing until well combined. Chill dough for at least 2 hours, I like to chill overnight.
2. Preheat the oven to 375 degrees F (190 degrees C). Grease cookie sheets. On a lightly floured surface, roll dough out to 1/4 inch thick. Cut into desired shapes using cookie cutters. Place cookies 1 inch apart on the prepared cookie sheets.
3. Bake for 10 to 12 minutes in the preheated oven, until cookies are firm and lightly toasted on the edges.

GINGERBREAD BISCOTTI

Servings: 48 | Prep: 25m | Cooks: 40m | Total: 1h5m

NUTRITION FACTS

Calories: 70 | Carbohydrates: 12.1g | Fat: 2g | Protein: 1.4g | Cholesterol: 12mg

INGREDIENTS

* 1/3 cup vegetable oil
* 1 tablespoon baking powder
* 1 cup white sugar
* 1 1/2 tablespoons ground ginger
* 3 eggs
* 3/4 tablespoon ground cinnamon
* 1/4 cup molasses
* 1/2 tablespoon ground cloves
* 2 1/4 cups all-purpose flour
* 1/4 teaspoon ground nutmeg
* 1 cup whole wheat flour

DIRECTIONS

1. Preheat the oven to 375 degrees F (190 degrees C). Grease a cookie sheet.
2. In a large bowl, mix together oil, sugar, eggs, and molasses. In another bowl, combine flours, baking powder, ginger, cinnamon, cloves, and nutmeg; mix into egg mixture to form a stiff dough.

3. Divide dough in half, and shape each half into a roll the length of the cookie. Place rolls on cookie sheet, and pat down to flatten the dough to 1/2 inch thickness.
4. Bake in preheated oven for 25 minutes. Remove from oven, and set aside to cool.
5. When cool enough to touch, cut into 1/2 inch thick diagonal slices. Place sliced biscotti on cookie sheet, and bake an additional 5 to 7 minutes on each side, or until toasted and crispy.

CRANBERRY BARS

Servings: 24 | Prep: 30m | Cooks: 40m | Total: 1h10m

NUTRITION FACTS

Calories: 228 | Carbohydrates: 36.1g | Fat: 8.9g | Protein: 2g | Cholesterol: 31mg

INGREDIENTS

- 1 (12 ounce) package whole cranberries
- 2 eggs
- 1 cup white sugar
- 1 cup rolled oats
- 3/4 cup water
- 3/4 cup packed light brown sugar
- 1 (18.25 ounce) package yellow cake mix
- 1 teaspoon ground ginger
- 3/4 cup butter, melted
- 1 teaspoon ground cinnamon

DIRECTIONS

1. In a saucepan over medium heat, combine the cranberries, white sugar, and water. Cook, stirring occasionally until all of the cranberries have popped, and the mixture is thick, about 15 minutes. Remove from heat, and set aside to cool.
2. Preheat the oven to 350 degrees F (175 degrees C).
3. In a large bowl, mix together the cake mix, melted butter, and eggs. Stir in the oats, brown sugar, ginger and cinnamon. Set aside about 1 1/2 cups of the mixture, and spread the rest into the bottom of a 9x13 inch baking dish. Pack down to form a solid crust, getting it as even as possible. Spread the cooled cranberry mixture over the crust. Pinch off pieces of the remaining mixture and place evenly over the cranberry layer.
4. Bake for 35 to 40 minutes in the preheated oven, until the top is lightly browned. Cool in the pan for about 40 minutes before slicing into bars.

CITRUS SHORTBREAD COOKIES

Servings: 24 | Prep: 25m | Cooks: 10m | Total: 4h35m | Additional: 4h

NUTRITION FACTS

Calories: 153 | Carbohydrates: 20.2g | Fat: g | Protein: 1.2g | Cholesterol: 20mg

INGREDIENTS

- 2 cups all-purpose flour
- 2 teaspoons vanilla extract
- 1/4 teaspoon baking powder
- 1/2 teaspoon almond extract
- 1/8 teaspoon salt
- 1 tablespoon grated orange zest, or more to taste
- 1 cup butter, softened
- 2 cups sweetened dried cranberries, chopped
- 3/4 cup confectioners' sugar

DIRECTIONS

1. Combine flour, baking powder, and salt in a bowl; set aside. Beat the butter and confectioners' sugar with an electric mixer in a large bowl until smooth. Stir in the vanilla and almond extracts and orange zest. Mix in the flour mixture until just incorporated. Fold in the cranberries; mixing just enough to evenly combine.
2. Divide the dough into 2 equal portions, then roll into logs about 7 inches long. Wrap each log in wax paper or plastic wrap, and chill in the refrigerator for at least 4 hours.
3. Preheat an oven to 350 degrees F (175 degrees C).
4. Remove wax paper, and cut the cookie dough into 1/2-inch slices. Arrange the slices on a baking sheet about 1 inch apart.
5. Bake in the preheated oven until firm but not browned, about 10 minutes.

GRANDMA MINNIE'S OLD FASHIONED SUGAR COOKIES

Servings: 78 | Prep: 20m | Cooks: 8m | Total: 28m

NUTRITION FACTS

Calories: 51 | Carbohydrates: 6.3g | Fat: g | Protein: 0.6g | Cholesterol: 9mg

INGREDIENTS

- 3 cups sifted all-purpose flour
- 1 cup butter
- 1 1/2 teaspoons baking powder
- 1 egg, lightly beaten
- 1/2 teaspoon salt
- 3 tablespoons cream

- 1 cup white sugar
- 1 teaspoon vanilla extract

DIRECTIONS

1. Preheat oven to 400 degrees F (200 degrees C) .
2. Over a large bowl, sift together all-purpose flour, baking powder, salt, sugar. Cut in butter and blend with a pastry blender until mixture resembles cornmeal. Stir in lightly beaten egg, cream, and vanilla. Blend well. Dough may be chilled, if desired.
3. On a floured surface, roll out dough to 1/8 inch thickness. Sprinkle with sugar; cut into desired shapes. Transfer to ungreased baking sheets.
4. Bake for 6 to 8 minutes, or until delicately brown.

NANAIMO BARS

Servings: 16 | Prep: 30m | Cooks: 0m | Total: 30m

NUTRITION FACTS

Calories: 311 | Carbohydrates: 34.1g | Fat: 19.6g | Protein: 2.8g | Cholesterol: 47mg

INGREDIENTS

- 1/2 cup butter, softened
- 1/2 cup butter, softened
- 1/4 cup white sugar
- 3 tablespoons heavy cream
- 5 tablespoons unsweetened cocoa powder
- 2 tablespoons custard powder
- 1 egg, beaten
- 2 cups confectioners' sugar
- 1 3/4 cups graham cracker crumbs
- 4 (1 ounce) squares semisweet baking chocolate
- 1 cup flaked coconut
- 2 teaspoons butter
- 1/2 cup finely chopped almonds (optional)

DIRECTIONS

1. In the top of a double boiler, combine 1/2 cup butter, white sugar and cocoa powder. Stir occasionally until melted and smooth. Beat in the egg, stirring until thick, 2 to 3 minutes. Remove from heat and mix in the graham cracker crumbs, coconut and almonds (if you like). Press into the bottom of an ungreased 8x8 inch pan.

2. For the middle layer, cream together 1/2 cup butter, heavy cream and custard powder until light and fluffy. Mix in the confectioners' sugar until smooth. Spread over the bottom layer in the pan. Chill to set.

3. While the second layer is chilling, melt the semisweet chocolate and 2 teaspoons butter together in the microwave or over low heat. Spread over the chilled bars. Let the chocolate set before cutting into squares.

APRICOT CREAM CHEESE THUMBPRINTS
Servings: 84 | Prep: 15m | Cooks: 15m | Total: 2h30m | Additional: 2h

NUTRITION FACTS

Calories: 89 | Carbohydrates: 11.8g | Fat: 4.4g | Protein: 1.1g | Cholesterol: 16mg

INGREDIENTS

- 1 1/2 cups butter, softened
- 1 1/2 teaspoons lemon zest
- 1 1/2 cups white sugar
- 4 1/2 cups all-purpose flour
- 1 (8 ounce) package cream cheese, softened
- 1 1/2 teaspoons baking powder
- 2 eggs
- 1 cup apricot preserves
- 2 tablespoons lemon juice
- 1/3 cup confectioners' sugar for decoration

DIRECTIONS

1. In a large bowl, cream together the butter, sugar, and cream cheese until smooth. Beat in the eggs one at a time, then stir in the lemon juice and lemon zest. Combine the flour and baking powder; stir into the cream cheese mixture until just combined. Cover, and chill until firm, about 1 hour.

2. Preheat oven to 350 degrees F (175 degrees C). Roll tablespoonfuls of dough into balls, and place them 2 inches apart on ungreased cookie sheets. Using your finger, make an indention in the center of each ball, and fill with 1/2 teaspoon of apricot preserves.

3. Bake for 15 minutes in the preheated oven, or until edges are golden. Allow cookies to cool on the baking sheets for 2 minutes before removing to wire racks to cool completely. Sprinkle with confectioner's sugar.

SUGAR COOKIES WITH BUTTERCREAM FROSTING
Servings: 60 | Prep: 15m | Cooks: 5m | Total: 2h20m | Additional: 2h

NUTRITION FACTS

Calories: 112 | Carbohydrates: 16.1g | Fat: 5g | Protein: 0.9g | Cholesterol: 14 mg

INGREDIENTS

- 1 cup butter
- 1/2 teaspoon salt
- 1 cup white sugar
- 1/2 cup shortening
- 2 eggs
- 1 pound confectioners' sugar
- 1/2 teaspoon vanilla extract
- 5 tablespoons water
- 3 1/4 cups all-purpose flour
- 1/4 teaspoon salt
- 1/2 teaspoon baking powder
- 1/2 teaspoon vanilla extract
- 1/2 teaspoon baking soda
- 1/4 teaspoon butter flavored extract

DIRECTIONS

1. In a large bowl, mix together butter, sugar, eggs, and vanilla with an electric mixer until light and fluffy. Combine the flour, baking powder, baking soda, and salt; gradually stir flour mixture into butter mixture until well blended using a sturdy spoon. Chill dough for 2 hours.
2. Preheat the oven to 400 degrees F (200 degrees C). On a lightly floured surface, roll out the dough to 1/4 inch thickness. Cut into desired shapes using cookie cutters. Place cookies 2 inches apart onto ungreased cookie sheets.
3. Bake for 4 to 6 minutes in the preheated oven. Remove cookies from pan and cool on wire racks.
4. Using an electric mixer, beat shortening, confectioners sugar, water, salt, vanilla extract, and butter flavoring until fluffy. Frost cookies after they have cooled completely.

PECAN TURTLES BARS

Servings: 48 | Prep: 20m | Cooks: 25m | Total: 1h15m | Additional: 30m

NUTRITION FACTS

Calories: 114 | Carbohydrates: 12.1g | Fat: 7.3g | Protein: 0.9g | Cholesterol: 13mg

INGREDIENTS

- 1 1/2 cups all-purpose flour
- 1 cup pecan halves
- 1 1/2 cups brown sugar, divided
- 2/3 cup butter

- 1/2 cup butter, softened
- 1 cup milk chocolate chips

DIRECTIONS

1. Preheat oven to 350 degrees F (175 degrees C).
2. Combine flour, 1 cup brown sugar, and softened butter in large mixer bowl. Beat at medium speed for 2 to 3 minutes or until mixture resembles fine crumbs. Pat mixture evenly onto bottom of ungreased 13x9-inch baking pan. Sprinkle pecans evenly over crumb mixture.
3. Combine 2/3 cup butter and remaining 1/2 cup brown sugar in small saucepan. Cook and stir over medium heat until entire surface is bubbly; cook, stirring constantly, 1/2 to 1 minute more. Pour into pan, spreading evenly over crust.
4. Bake in preheated oven until entire surface is bubbly, 18 to 20 minutes. Remove from oven; immediately sprinkle with chocolate pieces. Let stand 2 to 3 minutes to allow chocolate to melt; use a knife or small spatula to swirl chocolate slightly. Cool completely in pan on a wire rack. Use sharp knife to cut into 48 bars.

CREAM CHEESE KOLACKY

Servings: 30 | Prep: 15m | Cooks: 10m | Total: 3h25m | Additional: 3h

NUTRITION FACTS

Calories: 72 | Carbohydrates: 8.2g | Fat: 4.1g | Protein: 0.7g | Cholesterol: 11mg

INGREDIENTS

- 3 ounces cream cheese
- 1/2 cup any flavor fruit jam
- 1/2 cup butter, softened
- 1/3 cup confectioners' sugar for decoration
- 1 cup all-purpose flour

DIRECTIONS

1. Mix cream cheese and butter until smooth. Add flour slowly until well blended. Shape into a ball and chill overnight or for several hours.
2. Preheat oven to 350 degrees F (180 degrees C).
3. Roll dough out 1/8 inch thick on a floured pastry board. Cut into 2 1/2 inch squares and place about 1/2 teaspoon jam or preserves in the center. Overlap opposite corners and pinch together. Place on ungreased cookie sheets.
4. Bake for 10 to 12 minutes in the preheated oven. Cool on wire racks. Sprinkle kolacky lightly with confectioner's sugar.

MACARON (FRENCH MACAROON)

Servings: 8 | Prep: 30m | Cooks: 10m | Total: 2h10m | Additional: 1h30m

NUTRITION FACTS

Calories: 189 | Carbohydrates: 36.4g | Fat: 2.6g | Protein: 6.9g | Cholesterol: 0mg

INGREDIENTS

- 3 egg whites
- 1 2/3 cups confectioners' sugar
- 1/4 cup white sugar
- 1 cup finely ground almonds

DIRECTIONS

1. Line a baking sheet with a silicone baking mat.
2. Beat egg whites in the bowl of a stand mixer fitted with a whisk attachment until whites are foamy; beat in white sugar and continue beating until egg whites are glossy, fluffy, and hold soft peaks. Sift confectioners' sugar and ground almonds in a separate bowl and quickly fold the almond mixture into the egg whites, about 30 strokes.
3. Spoon a small amount of batter into a plastic bag with a small corner cut off and pipe a test disk of batter, about 1 1/2 inches in diameter, onto prepared baking sheet. If the disk of batter holds a peak instead of flattening immediately, gently fold the batter a few more times and retest.
4. When batter is mixed enough to flatten immediately into an even disk, spoon into a pastry bag fitted with a plain round tip. Pipe the batter onto the baking sheet in rounds, leaving space between the disks. Let the piped cookies stand out at room temperature until they form a hard skin on top, about 1 hour.
5. Preheat oven to 285 degrees F (140 degrees C).
6. Bake cookies until set but not browned, about 10 minutes; let cookies cool completely before filling.

COWBOY COOKIE MIX IN A JAR

Servings: 18 | Prep: 25m | Cooks: 0m | Total: 25m

NUTRITION FACTS

Calories: 167 | Carbohydrates: 29.1g | Fat: 5.5g | Protein: 2.4g | Cholesterol: 0mg

INGREDIENTS

- 1 1/3 cups rolled oats
- 1 1/3 cups all-purpose flour
- 1/2 cup packed brown sugar
- 1 teaspoon baking powder

- 1/2 cup white sugar
- 1 teaspoon baking soda
- 1/2 cup chopped pecans
- 1/4 teaspoon salt
- 1 cup semisweet chocolate chips

DIRECTIONS

1. Layer the ingredients in a 1 quart jar in the order given. Press each layer firmly in place before adding the next layer.
2. Include a card with the following instructions: Cowboy Cookie Mix in a Jar 1. Preheat oven to 350 degrees F (175 degrees C). Grease cookie sheets. 2. In a medium bowl, mix together 1/2 cup melted butter or margarine, 1 egg, and 1 teaspoon of vanilla. Stir in the entire contents of the jar. You may need to use your hands to finish mixing. Shape into walnut sized balls. Place 2 inches apart on prepared cookie sheets. 3. Bake for 11 to 13 minutes in the preheated oven. Transfer from cookie sheets to cool on wire racks.

CHOCOLATE CARAMEL BROWNIES

Servings: 15 | Prep: 15m | Cooks: 15m | Total: 30m

NUTRITION FACTS

Calories: 460 | Carbohydrates: 64.1g | Fat: 22.1g | Protein: 5.6g | Cholesterol: 35mg

INGREDIENTS

- 14 ounces caramels
- 3/4 cup butter, melted
- 1/2 cup evaporated milk
- 1/4 cup chopped pecans
- 1 (18.25 ounce) package German chocolate cake mix
- 2 cups milk chocolate chi
- 1/3 cup evaporated milk

DIRECTIONS

1. Peel caramels and place in a microwave-safe bowl. Stir in 1/2 cup evaporated milk. Heat and stir until all caramels are melted.
2. Preheat oven to 350 degrees F (175 degrees C) Grease a 9x13 inch pan.
3. In a large mixing bowl, mix together cake mix, 1/3 cup evaporated milk, melted butter, and chopped pecans. Place 1/2 of the batter in prepared baking pan.
4. Bake for 8 minutes.
5. Place the remaining batter into the fridge. Remove brownies from oven and sprinkle chocolate chips on top. Drizzle caramel sauce over chocolate chips. Remove brownie mix from refrigerator. Using a

teaspoon, make small balls with the batter and smash flat. Very carefully, place on top of the caramel sauce until the top is completely covered.

6. Bake for an additional 20 minutes. Remove and let cool.

GINGERBREAD COOKIES

Servings: 72 | Prep: 20m | Cooks: 12m | Total: 4h | Additional: 3h28m

NUTRITION FACTS

Calories: 90 | Carbohydrates: 14.5g | Fat: 3g | Protein: 1.2g | Cholesterol: 3mg

INGREDIENTS

- 6 cups all-purpose flour
- 1 cup shortening, melted and cooled slightly
- 1 tablespoon baking powder
- 1 cup molasses
- 1 tablespoon ground ginger
- 1 cup packed brown sugar
- 1 teaspoon ground nutmeg
- 1/2 cup water
- 1 teaspoon ground cloves
- 1 egg
- 1 teaspoon ground cinnamon
- 1 teaspoon vanilla extract

DIRECTIONS

1. Sift together the flour, baking powder, ginger, nutmeg, cloves, and cinnamon; set aside.
2. In a medium bowl, mix together the shortening, molasses, brown sugar, water, egg, and vanilla until smooth. Gradually stir in the dry ingredients, until they are completely absorbed. Divide dough into 3 pieces, pat down to 1 1/2 inch thickness, wrap in plastic wrap, and refrigerate for at least 3 hours.
3. Preheat oven to 350 degrees F (175 degrees C). On a lightly floured surface, roll the dough out to 1/4 inch thickness. Cut into desired shapes with cookie cutters. Place cookies 1 inch apart onto an ungreased cookie sheet.
4. Bake for 10 to 12 minutes in the preheated oven. When the cookies are done, they will look dry, but still be soft to the touch. Remove from the baking sheet to cool on wire racks. When cool, the cookies can be frosted with the icing of your choice.

BLUE RIBBON SUGAR COOKIES

Servings: 48 | Prep: 35m | Cooks: 25m | Total: 1h

NUTRITION FACTS

INGREDIENTS

- 3/4 cup butter, softened
- 1 1/2 teaspoons lemon extract
- 1 cup vegetable oil
- 4 cups all-purpose flour
- 1 cup confectioners' sugar
- 1 teaspoon cream of tartar
- 1 cup white sugar
- 1 teaspoon baking soda
- 2 eggs
- 1 teaspoon salt
- 1 teaspoon vanilla extract
- 1/2 cup white sugar for decoration

DIRECTIONS

1. Preheat the oven to 375 degrees F (190 degrees C). Sift together the flour, cream of tartar, baking soda and salt; set aside.
2. In a large bowl, cream together the butter, oil, confectioners' sugar and white sugar until well blended. Stir in the eggs, vanilla and lemon extracts. Gradually mix in the dry ingredients until well blended. Roll the dough into walnut sized balls. Place the cookies 2 inches apart onto the cookie sheet. Flatten cookies to 1/8 inch thickness using the bottom of a glass dipped in sugar. Colored sugar may be used if you do not plan to frost cookies later.
3. Bake for 9 to 12 minutes in the preheated oven, or until the edges are golden brown. Allow cookies to cool on baking sheet for 5 minutes before removing to a wire rack to cool completely.

WHOLE WHEAT GINGER SNAPS

Servings: 60 | Prep: 10m | Cooks: 15m | Total: 25m

NUTRITION FACTS

Calories: 106 | Carbohydrates: 18.5g | Fat: 3.4g | Protein: 1.4g | Cholesterol: 14mg

INGREDIENTS

- 1 cup butter or margarine
- 1 tablespoon ground ginger
- 1 1/2 cups white sugar
- 1 1/2 teaspoons ground nutmeg
- 2 eggs, beaten
- 1 1/2 teaspoons ground cinnamon

- 1 cup molasses
- 1 1/2 teaspoons ground cloves
- 4 cups whole wheat flour
- 1 1/2 teaspoons ground allspice
- 1 tablespoon baking soda
- 1 cup white sugar for decoration
- 2 teaspoons baking powder

DIRECTIONS

1. Preheat the oven to 350 degrees F (175 degrees C). Grease cookie sheets.
2. In a large bowl, cream together the butter and 1 1/2 cups of sugar until smooth. Mix in the eggs, and then the molasses. Combine the whole wheat flour, baking soda, baking powder, ginger, nutmeg, cinnamon, cloves, and allspice, heaping the measures if you like a lot of spice. Stir the dry ingredients into the molasses mixture just until blended.
3. Roll the dough into small balls, and dip the top of each ball into the remaining white sugar. Place the cookies about 2 inches apart on the cookie sheets.
4. Bake for 10 to 15 minutes in the preheated oven, until the tops are cracked. Bake longer for crispy cookies, less time for chewy cookies. Cool on wire racks.

FRESH GINGER COOKIES

Servings: 30 | Prep: 30m | Cooks: 15m | Total: 1h45m | Additional: 1h

NUTRITION FACTS

Calories: 137 | Carbohydrates: 22.6g | Fat: 4.9g | Protein: 1.2g | Cholesterol: 18mg

INGREDIENTS

- 2 1/4 cups all-purpose flour
- 1 cup white sugar
- 1 teaspoon baking soda
- 1/4 cup molasses
- 1/2 teaspoon salt
- 1 egg
- 2 tablespoons grated fresh ginger
- 1 cup white sugar
- 3/4 cup butter, softened

DIRECTIONS

1. In a large mixing bowl, combine flour, soda, and salt. In a separate bowl, beat ginger, butter, and 1 cup sugar until light and fluffy. Beat in molasses and egg. Gently fold in flour mixture until just combined. Chill for 1 hour.

2. Preheat oven to 350 degrees F (175 degrees C).
3. Roll dough into 1 1/2 inch balls and then roll them in sugar. Place 2 inches apart on ungreased baking sheets.
4. Bake until edges start to brown, about 15 minutes. Centers will be slightly soft. Let stand on cookie sheets 1 minute and remove to racks to cool completely.

MAPLE PECAN SHORTBREAD SQUARES

Servings: 16 | Prep: 10m | Cooks: 35m | Total: 2h15m | Additional: 1h30m

NUTRITION FACTS

Calories: 152 | Carbohydrates: 18g | Fat: 8.6g | Protein: 1.6g | Cholesterol: 27mg

INGREDIENTS

- 1 cup all-purpose flour
- 1/3 cup packed brown sugar
- 1/3 cup packed brown sugar
- 3 tablespoons pure maple syrup
- 1/2 cup softened butter
- 1/2 cup chopped pecans
- 1 egg

DIRECTIONS

1. Preheat an oven to 350 degrees F (175 degrees C).
2. Combine the flour and 1/3 cup brown sugar in a mixer. Mix in the softened butter until a dough has formed. Press into an ungreased 8x8-inch baking dish, and prick with a fork.
3. Bake the shortbread in the preheated oven until golden brown, about 20 minutes. While the shortbread is baking, beat the egg in a mixing bowl along with 1/3 cup brown sugar, maple syrup, and pecans. Pour the pecan mixture over the hot crust, and return to the oven. Continue baking until firmed, 12 to 15 minutes. Remove from the oven, and immediately run a knife around the edges to prevent sticking. Cool completely, then cut into 1-inch squares to serve.

RUM OR BOURBON BALLS

Servings: 24 | Prep: 10m | Cooks: 2m | Total: 1h | Additional: 1h

NUTRITION FACTS

Calories: 194 | Carbohydrates: 26g | Fat: 8.9g | Protein: 1.8g | Cholesterol: 0mg

INGREDIENTS

- 1 cup semisweet chocolate chips

- 2 1/2 cups crushed vanilla wafers
- 1/2 cup white sugar
- 1 cup chopped walnuts (optional)
- 3 tablespoons corn syrup
- 1/3 cup confectioners' sugar
- 1/2 cup rum

DIRECTIONS

1. Place chocolate chips into a microwave-safe medium bowl. Heat in the microwave for 1 minute, stir and then continue to heat at 20 second intervals, stirring between each, until melted and smooth. Stir in sugar and corn syrup. Blend in rum. Add crushed vanilla wafers and chopped nuts. Mix until evenly distributed. Cover and refrigerate until firm.
2. Roll the chilled chocolate mixture into bite-size balls. Roll balls in a mixture of ground nuts and confectioner's sugar, or just plain confectioner's sugar. Store in a covered container for a week before serving to blend the flavors.

AMY'S CHOCOLATE CHIP COOKIES

Servings: 24 | Prep: 5m | Cooks: 10m | Total: 15m

NUTRITION FACTS

Calories: 236 | Carbohydrates: 30.8g | Fat: 12.1g | Protein: 2.8g | Cholesterol: 16mg

INGREDIENTS

- 2 1/4 cups all-purpose flour
- 1 teaspoon vanilla extract
- 1 teaspoon baking soda
- 1 (3.5 ounce) package instant vanilla pudding mix
- 1 cup margarine, softened
- 2 eggs
- 1/4 cup white sugar
- 2 cups semisweet chocolate chips
- 3/4 cup packed light brown sugar

DIRECTIONS

1. Preheat oven to 375 degrees F (190 degrees C).
2. In a medium-sized mixing bowl, combine flour and baking soda. Set aside. In another large mixing bowl, combine butter, white sugar, brown sugar, vanilla, and pudding mix. Beat until smooth and creamy. Beat in eggs. Gradually stir in flour mixture. Stir in chocolate chips.
3. Drop batter by heaping teaspoonfuls, about 2 inches apart, onto an ungreased cookie sheet. Bake for 9 to 9 1/2 minutes, or until browned.

PEPPERMINT PATTIES

Servings: 28 | Prep: 45m | Cooks: 10m | Total: 2h55m | Additional: 2h

NUTRITION FACTS

Calories: 183 | Carbohydrates: 32.9g | Fat: 6.5g | Protein: 1.4g | Cholesterol: 3mg

INGREDIENTS

- 3/4 cup sweetened condensed milk
- 3 cups semisweet chocolate chips
- 1 1/2 teaspoons peppermint extract
- 2 teaspoons shortening
- 4 cups confectioners' sugar

DIRECTIONS

1. In a large mixing bowl, combine condensed milk and peppermint extract. Beat in enough confectioners' sugar, a little at a time, to form a stiff dough that is no longer sticky. Form into 1 inch balls, then place on waxed paper and flatten with fingers to form patties. Let patties dry at room temperature two hours, turning once.
2. In a medium saucepan over low heat, melt chocolate with shortening, stirring often. Remove from heat. Dip patties, one at a time, into chocolate by laying them on the tines of a fork and lowering the fork into the liquid. Let cool on waxed paper until set.

SOFT GINGERBREAD COOKIES

Servings: 36 | Prep: 25m | Cooks: 10m | Total: 3h45m | Additional: 3h10m

NUTRITION FACTS

Calories: 75 | Carbohydrates: 15.8g | Fat: 0.8g | Protein: 1.2g | Cholesterol: 2mg

INGREDIENTS

- 3/4 cup molasses
- 1 teaspoon baking soda
- 1/3 cup packed brown sugar
- 1/2 teaspoon ground allspice
- 1/3 cup water
- 1 teaspoon ground ginger
- 1/8 cup butter, softened
- 1/2 teaspoon ground cloves
- 3 1/4 cups all-purpose flour
- 1/2 teaspoon ground cinnamon

DIRECTIONS

1. In a medium bowl, mix together the molasses, brown sugar, water and butter until smooth. Combine the flour, baking soda, allspice, ginger, cloves and cinnamon, stir them into the wet mixture until all of the dry is absorbed. Cover the dough and chill for at least 3 hours.
2. Preheat oven to 350 degrees F (175 degrees C). On a lightly floured surface, roll the dough out to 1/4 inch thickness. Cut out into desired shapes. Place cookies 1 inch apart onto ungreased cookie sheets.
3. Bake for 8 to 10 minutes in the preheated oven. Remove from the cookie sheets to cool on wire racks.

CHRISTMAS WREATHS

Servings: 18 | Prep: 5m | Cooks: 10m | Total: 30m | Additional: 15m

NUTRITION FACTS

Calories: 112 | Carbohydrates: 16.7g | Fat: 5.2g | Protein: 0.7g | Cholesterol: 14mg

INGREDIENTS

- 1/2 cup butter
- 1 teaspoon vanilla extract
- 30 large marshmallows
- 4 cups cornflakes cereal
- 1 1/2 teaspoons green food coloring
- 2 tablespoons cinnamon red hot candies

DIRECTIONS

1. Melt butter in a large saucepan over low heat. Add marshmallows, and cook until melted, stirring constantly. Remove from heat, and stir in the food coloring, vanilla, and cornflakes.
2. Quickly drop heaping tablespoonfuls of the mixture onto waxed paper, and form into a wreath shape with lightly greased fingers. Immediately decorate with red hot candies. Allow to cool to room temperature before removing from waxed paper, and storing in an airtight container.

SNOW FLAKES

Servings: 72 | Prep: 20m | Cooks: 10m | Total: 1h | Additional: 30m

NUTRITION FACTS

Calories: 58 | Carbohydrates: 6.1g | Fat: g | Protein: 0.6g | Cholesterol: 4mg

INGREDIENTS

- 1 cup butter flavored shortening

- 1 teaspoon orange zest
- 1 (3 ounce) package cream cheese, softened
- 2 1/2 cups all-purpose flour
- 1 cup white sugar
- 1/2 teaspoon salt
- 1 egg yolk
- 1/4 teaspoon ground cinnamon
- 1 teaspoon vanilla extract

DIRECTIONS

1. Preheat oven to 350 degrees F (175 degrees C).
2. In a medium bowl, cream together shortening, cream cheese, and sugar. Beat in egg yolk, vanilla, and orange zest. Continue beating until light and fluffy. Gradually stir in flour, salt, and cinnamon. Fill the cookie press, and form cookies on ungreased cookie sheet.
3. Bake in preheated oven for 10 to 12 minutes. Remove from cookie sheet, and cool on wire racks.

MARY'S SUGAR COOKIES

Servings: 30 | Prep: 15m | Cooks: 8m | Total: 2h25m | Additional: 2h2m

NUTRITION FACTS

Calories: 126 | Carbohydrates: 16g | Fat: 6.4g | Protein: 1.4g | Cholesterol: 22mg

INGREDIENTS

- 1 cup butter, softened
- 2 1/2 cups all-purpose flour
- 1 1/2 cups sifted confectioners' sugar
- 1 teaspoon baking soda
- 1 egg
- 1 teaspoon cream of tartar
- 1 teaspoon vanilla extract
- 1/4 cup granulated sugar for decoration
- 1/2 teaspoon almond extract

DIRECTIONS

1. In a large bowl, cream together the butter and confectioners' sugar until smooth. Beat in the egg and stir in the vanilla and almond extract. Combine the flour, baking soda and cream of tartar; blend into the creamed mixture. Cover and chill for at least two hours.
2. Preheat the oven to 375 degrees F (190 degrees C). Divide the dough into two parts. On a lightly floured surface, roll each piece of the dough out to 3/16 inch in thickness. Cut into desired shapes

with cookie cutters. Place cookies 1 1/2 inches apart onto greased cookie sheets. Sprinkle cookies with plain or colored granulated sugar.

3. Bake for 8 minutes in the preheated oven, until lightly browned. Allow cookies to cool on baking sheet for 5 minutes before removing to a wire rack to cool completely.

PEBBER NODDER (DANISH CHRISTMAS COOKIES)
Servings: 100 | Prep: 15m | Cooks: 10m | Total: 25m

NUTRITION FACTS

Calories: 37 | Carbohydrates: 4.4g | Fat: 2g | Protein: 0.5g | Cholesterol: 9mg

INGREDIENTS

- 1 cup butter
- 2 1/2 cups all-purpose flour
- 1 cup sugar
- 1 teaspoon ground cardamom
- 2 eggs
- 1 teaspoon ground cinnamon, or to taste

DIRECTIONS

1. Preheat the oven to 350 degrees F (175 degrees C).
2. In a large bowl, mix together the butter and sugar until smooth. Beat in the eggs one at a time, stirring until light and fluffy. Combine the flour, cardamom and cinnamon; stir into the sugar mixture just until blended.
3. Separate the dough into 6 balls, and roll each ball into a rope about as big around as your finger on a lightly floured surface. Cut into 1/2-inch pieces, and place them on an ungreased baking sheet.
4. Bake for 10 minutes in the preheated oven, or until lightly browned. Cool on baking sheets for a few minutes, then transfer to wire racks to cool completely.

EGGNOG THUMBPRINTSO
Servings: 48 | Prep: 20m | Cooks: 12m | Total: 1h | Additional: 28m

NUTRITION FACTS

Calories: 77 | Carbohydrates: 9.7g | Fat: 4g | Protein: 0.7g | Cholesterol: 14mg

INGREDIENTS

- 3/4 cup butter, softened
- 1/4 teaspoon salt
- 1/2 cup white sugar

- 1/4 cup butter
- 1/4 cup packed brown sugar
- 1 cup confectioners' sugar
- 1 egg
- 1 tablespoon rum
- 1/2 teaspoon vanilla extract
- 1 pinch ground nutme
- 2 cups all-purpose flour

DIRECTIONS

1. Preheat the oven to 350 degrees F (175 degrees C).
2. In a medium bowl, cream together 3/4 cup butter, white sugar, and brown sugar until smooth. Beat in egg and vanilla. Combine flour and salt; stir into the creamed mixture by hand to form a soft dough. Roll dough into 1 inch balls, and place balls 2 inches apart on ungreased cookie sheets. Make an indention in the center of each cookie using your finger or thumb.
3. Bake for 12 minutes in preheated oven. Cool completely.
4. In a small bowl, mix together 1/4 cup butter, confectioners' sugar, and rum. Spoon rounded teaspoonfuls of filling onto cookies. Sprinkle with nutmeg. Let stand until set before storing in an airtight container.

JAM KOLACHES

Servings: 12 | Prep: 45m | Cooks: 15m | Total: 1h

NUTRITION FACTS

Calories: 168 | Carbohydrates: 17.3g | Fat: 10.3g | Protein: 2g | Cholesterol: 28mg

INGREDIENTS

- 1/2 cup butter, softened
- 1/4 cup strawberry jam
- 3 ounces cream cheese, softened
- 1/4 cup sifted confectioners' sugar
- 1 1/4 cups all-purpose flour

DIRECTIONS

1. Beat butter and cream cheese in mixer bowl until light and fluffy. Add flour gradually, beating well after each addition.
2. Roll dough to 1/8 inch thickness on lightly floured surface. Cut into 2-inch circles. Spoon 1/4 teaspoon jam into center of each circle. Fold opposite edges together, slightly overlapping edges.
3. Place 2 inches apart on greased cookie sheet. Bake at 375 degrees F (190 degrees C) for 15 minutes. Remove to wire rack to cool. Sprinkle with confectioners' sugar.

GREEK BUTTER COOKIES

Servings: 48 | Prep: 10m | Cooks: 10m | Total: 20m

NUTRITION FACTS

Calories: 74 | Carbohydrates: 8.9g | Fat: 4g | Protein: 0.8g | Cholesterol: 14mg

INGREDIENTS

- 1 cup butter, softened
- 1/2 teaspoon almond extract
- 3/4 cup white sugar
- 2 1/4 cups all-purpose flour
- 1 egg
- 1/2 cup confectioners' sugar for rolling
- 1/2 teaspoon vanilla extract

DIRECTIONS

1. Preheat the oven to 400 degrees F (200 degrees C). Grease cookie sheets.
2. In a medium bowl, cream together the butter, sugar and egg until smooth. Stir in the vanilla and almond extracts. Blend in the flour to form a dough. you may have to knead by hand at the end. Take about a teaspoon of dough at a time and roll into balls, logs or 'S' shapes. Place cookies 1 to 2 inches apart onto the prepared cookie sheets.
3. Bake for 10 minutes in the preheated oven, or until lightly browned and firm. Allow cookies to cool completely before dusting with confectioners' sugar.

PFEFFERNUSSE COOKIES

Servings: 18 | Prep: 15m | Cooks: 15m | Total: 3h | Additional: 2h30m

NUTRITION FACTS

Calories: 284 | Carbohydrates: 53.9g | Fat: 6.3g | Protein: 3.7g | Cholesterol: 21mg

INGREDIENTS

- 1/2 cup molasses
- 1 teaspoon ground nutmeg
- 1/4 cup honey
- 1 teaspoon ground cloves
- 1/4 cup shortening
- 1 teaspoon ground ginger
- 1/4 cup margarine
- 2 teaspoons anise extract

- 2 eggs
- 2 teaspoons ground cinnamon
- 4 cups all-purpose flour
- 1 1/2 teaspoons baking soda
- 3/4 cup white sugar
- 1 teaspoon ground black pepper
- 1/2 cup brown sugar
- 1/2 teaspoon salt
- 1 1/2 teaspoons ground cardamom
- 1 cup confectioners' sugar for dusting
- 1/2 cup molasses

DIRECTIONS

1. Stir together the molasses, honey, shortening, and margarine in a saucepan over medium heat; cook and stir until creamy. Remove from heat and allow to cool to room temperature. Stir in the eggs.
2. Combine the flour, white sugar, brown sugar, cardamom, nutmeg, cloves, ginger, anise, cinnamon, baking soda, pepper, and salt in a large bowl. Add the molasses mixture and stir until thoroughly combines. Refrigerate at least 2 hours.
3. Preheat oven to 325 degrees F (165 degrees C). Roll the dough into acorn-sized balls. Arrange on baking sheets, spacing at least 1 inch apart.
4. Bake in preheated oven 10 to 15 minutes. Move to a rack to cool. Dust cooled cookies with confectioners' sugar.

BROWNIE MIX IN A JAR

Servings: 24 | Prep: 20m | Cooks: 0m | Total: 20m

NUTRITION FACTS

Calories: 118 | Carbohydrates: 25.4g | Fat: 2g | Protein: 1.3g | Cholesterol: 0mg

INGREDIENTS

- 1 1/4 cups all-purpose flour
- 2/3 cup unsweetened cocoa powder
- 1 teaspoon baking powder
- 2 1/4 cups white sugar
- 1 teaspoon salt
- 1/2 cup chopped pecans

DIRECTIONS

1. Mix together flour, baking powder, and salt in a quart jar. Layer remaining ingredients in the order listed. Press each layer firmly in place before adding the next layer. NOTE: Be sure to wipe out the

inside of the jar with a dry paper towel after adding the cocoa powder, so the other layers will show through the glass.

2. Attach a tag with the following instructions: Brownie Mix in a Jar 1. Preheat the oven to 350 degrees F (175 degrees C). Grease and flour a 9x13inch baking pan. 2. Empty jar of brownie mix into a large mixing bowl, and stir to blend. Mix in 3/4 cup melted butter and 4 eggs. Mix thoroughly. Spread batter evenly into prepared baking pan. 3. Bake for 25 to 30 minutes in preheated oven. Cool completely in pan before cutting into 2 inch squares.

ROSEMARY SHORTBREAD COOKIES
Servings: 36 | Prep: 1h20m | Cooks: 15m | Total: 1h35m

NUTRITION FACTS

Calories: 118 | Carbohydrates: 11.2g | Fat: 7.8g | Protein: 1.1g | Cholesterol: 20mg

INGREDIENTS

- 1 1/2 cups unsalted butter
- 2 3/4 cups all-purpose flour
- 2/3 cup white sugar
- 1/4 teaspoon salt
- 2 tablespoons chopped fresh rosemary
- 2 teaspoons white sugar for decoration

DIRECTIONS

1. In a medium bowl, cream together the butter and 2/3 cup of sugar until light and fluffy. Stir in the flour salt and rosemary until well blended. The dough will be somewhat soft. Cover and refrigerate for 1 hour.
2. Preheat the oven to 375 degrees F (190 degrees F). Line cookie sheets with parchment paper.
3. On a lightly floured surface, roll the dough out to 1/4 inch thickness. Cut into rectangles 1 1/2x2 inches in size. Place cookies 1 inch apart on the lined cookie sheets. Sprinkle the remaining sugar over the tops.
4. Bake for 8 minutes in the preheated oven, or until golden at the edges. Cool on wire racks, and store in an airtight container at room temperature.

COOKIE PRESS SHORTBREAD
Servings: 24 | Prep: 25m | Cooks: 10m | Total: 35m

NUTRITION FACTS

Calories: 116 | Carbohydrates: 10.9g | Fat: 7.8g | Protein: 0.9g | Cholesterol: 20mg

INGREDIENTS

- 1 cup butter
- 1/4 teaspoon vanilla extract
- 1 1/2 cups all-purpose flour
- 1/2 cup cornstarch
- 1/2 cup confectioners' sugar

DIRECTIONS

1. Preheat oven to 350 degrees F (175 degrees C).
2. In a medium mixing bowl, cream together butter, confectioners' sugar, and vanilla until smooth with electric mixer. Stir in flour and cornstarch. Pop dough into your cookie press, and away you go! Press cookies out onto ungreased cookie sheets.
3. Bake for 8 to 10 minutes in the preheated oven, or until the peaks are golden.

MERINGUE MUSHROOMS

Servings: 36 | Prep: 45m | Cooks: 1h | Total: 1h45m

NUTRITION FACTS

Calories: 39 | Carbohydrates: 7.1g | Fat: 1.3g | Protein: 0.6g | Cholesterol: 0mg

INGREDIENTS

- 1/2 cup egg whites
- 1 cup white sugar
- 1/4 teaspoon cream of tartar
- 1 tablespoon unsweetened cocoa powder
- 1/4 teaspoon salt
- 4 ounces chocolate confectioners' coating
- 1 teaspoon vanilla extract

DIRECTIONS

1. Preheat the oven to 225 degrees F (110 degrees C). Line 2 cookie sheets with parchment paper or aluminum foil.
2. In a large glass or metal bowl, use an electric mixer to whip egg whites until foamy. Add cream of tartar, salt, and vanilla. Continue whipping until the whites hold soft peaks. Gradually sprinkle in the sugar so that it does not sink to the bottom, and continue whipping until the mixture holds stiff shiny peaks.
3. Place a round tip into a pastry bag, and fill the bag half way with the meringue. To pipe the mushroom caps, squeeze out round mounds of meringue onto one of the prepared cookie sheets. Pull the bag off to the side to avoid making peaks on the top. For the stems, press out a tiny bit of

meringue onto the other sheet, then pull the bag straight up. They should resemble candy kisses. Do not worry about making all of the pieces exactly the same. The mushrooms will look more natural if the pieces are different sizes. Dust the mushroom caps lightly with cocoa using a small sifter or strainer.

4. Bake for 1 hour in the preheated oven, or until the caps are dry enough to easily remove from the cookie sheets. Set aside to cool completely. Melt the coating chocolate in a metal bowl over simmering water, or in a glass bowl in the microwave, stirring occasionally until smooth.
5. Poke a small hole in the bottom of a mushroom cap. Spread chocolate over the bottom of the cap. Dip the tip of a stem in chocolate, and press lightly into the hole. When the chocolate sets, they will hold together. Repeat with remaining pieces. Store at room temperature in a dry place or tin.

SHORTBREAD SUPREME

Servings: 12 | Prep: 25m | Cooks: 12m | Total: 37m

NUTRITION FACTS

Calories: 244 | Carbohydrates: 24.2g | Fat: 15.5g | Protein: 2.3g | Cholesterol: 41mg

INGREDIENTS

- 1 cup butter
- 1/2 cup white sugar
- 2 cups sifted all-purpose flour

DIRECTIONS

1. Preheat oven to 350 degrees F (175 degrees C).
2. In a medium bowl, beat the butter and sugar with an electric mixer until light and fluffy. Stir in flour by hand until the dough is smooth. Extra flour can be added if the dough is not stiff enough to roll out.
3. On a floured surface, roll dough to 1/4 inch thickness and cut into desired shapes with cookie cutters. Place 1 inch apart onto ungreased cookie sheets.
4. Bake for 12 to 15 minutes in the preheated oven, until the edges are lightly browned. Cool on cookie sheets for a few minutes before transferring to wire cooling racks.

DAWN'S EASY RED VELVET SANDWICH COOKIES

Servings: 24 | Prep: 25m | Cooks: 8m | Total: 33m

NUTRITION FACTS

Calories: 292 | Carbohydrates: 39.9g | Fat: 14.3g | Protein: 2.5g | Cholesterol: 29mg

INGREDIENTS

- 1 (18.25 ounce) box red velvet cake mix
- 2 teaspoons evaporated milk
- 2 eggs, lightly beaten
- 1 teaspoon vanilla
- 1/2 cup vegetable oil
- 1/2 cup flaked coconut
- 1 tablespoon bourbon
- 4 cups confectioners' sugar
- 1 (8 ounce) package cream cheese, softened
- 1/2 cup chopped pecans
- 1/4 cup butter, softened

DIRECTIONS

1. Preheat the oven to 375 degrees F (190 degrees C).
2. Mix together cake mix, eggs, oil, and bourbon in a large bowl. Roll the dough into balls the size of walnuts. Place 2 inches apart on ungreased baking sheets.
3. Bake in the preheated oven until the tops start to crack, about 8 minutes. Cool in the pans for 10 minutes before removing to cool completely on a wire rack.
4. In a large bowl combine cream cheese, butter, evaporated milk, vanilla, and coconut. Add the confectioners' sugar 1 cup at a time, mixing well with each addition. If consistency is too stiff, add more milk.
5. Place the chopped pecans in a bowl. Spread a generous amount of icing on the bottom of a cookie, sandwich it with another cookie, pressing firmly so that the icing comes all the way out to the edge. Roll the edges of the sandwich cookies in the chopped pecans. Repeat with the remaining cookies.

CLASSIC GINGERBREAD CUTOUTS

Servings: 36 | Prep: 30m | Cooks: 12m | Total: 1h | Additional: 18m

NUTRITION FACTS

Calories: 153 | Carbohydrates: 29.8g | Fat: 3g | Protein: 2.1g | Cholesterol: 17mg

INGREDIENTS

- 1/2 cup butter, softened
- 1/2 teaspoon ground allspice
- 1/2 cup brown sugar
- 1/2 teaspoon ground cloves
- 2/3 cup molasses
- 1/2 teaspoon ground cinnamon
- 2 eggs
- 1/2 teaspoon ground ginger

- 4 cups all-purpose flour, divided
- 1 pound confectioners' sugar
- 1/2 teaspoon baking soda
- 1/2 teaspoon cream of tartar
- 1/2 teaspoon salt
- 3 egg whites

DIRECTIONS

1. Preheat oven to 350 degrees F (175 degrees C).
2. In a large bowl, cream together the butter and brown sugar until smooth. Stir in the molasses and eggs. Combine 1 1/2 cups of the flour, baking soda, salt, allspice, cloves, cinnamon, and ginger; beat into the molasses mixture. Gradually stir in the remaining flour by hand to form a stiff dough.
3. Divide dough into 2 pieces. On a lightly floured surface, roll out dough to 1/8 inch thickness. Cut into desired shapes using cookie cutters. Place cookies 1 inch apart onto ungreased cookie sheets.
4. Bake for 8 to 10 minutes in the preheated oven. Allow cookies to cool on baking sheet for 5 minutes before removing to a wire rack to cool completely.
5. In a medium bowl, sift together confectioners' sugar and cream of tartar. Blend in egg whites. Using an electric mixer on high speed, beat for about 5 minutes, or until mixture is thick and stiff. Keep covered with a moist cloth until ready to frost cookies.

GINGERBREAD COOKIES

Servings: 60 | Prep: 30m | Cooks: 12m | Total: 1h | Additional: 18m

NUTRITION FACTS

Calories: 89 | Carbohydrates: 14.1g | Fat: 3.3g | Protein: 1g | Cholesterol: 1mg

INGREDIENTS

- 1 cup white sugar
- 2 teaspoons ground ginger
- 1 teaspoon ground nutmeg
- 1 teaspoon ground cinnamon
- 1/2 teaspoon salt
- 1 1/2 teaspoons baking soda
- 1 cup margarine, melted
- 1/2 cup evaporated milk
- 1 cup unsulfured molasses
- 3/4 teaspoon vanilla extract
- 3/4 teaspoon lemon extract
- 4 cups unbleached all-purpose flour

DIRECTIONS

1. Preheat oven to 375 degrees F (190 degrees C). Lightly grease cookie sheets.
2. In a large bowl, stir together the sugar, ginger, nutmeg, cinnamon, salt, and baking soda. Mix in the melted margarine, evaporated milk, molasses, vanilla, and lemon extracts. Stir in the flour, 1 cup at a time, mixing well after each addition. The dough should be stiff enough to handle without sticking to fingers. If necessary, increase flour by up to 1/2 cup to prevent sticking.
3. When the dough is smooth, roll it out to 1/4 inch thick on a floured surface, and cut into cookies. Place cookies on the prepared cookie sheets.
4. Bake for 10 to 12 minutes in the preheated oven. The cookies are done when the top springs back when touched. Remove from cookie sheets to cool on wire racks.

HOLLY CHRISTMAS COOKIES

Servings: 18 | Prep: 15m | Cooks: 10m | Total: 1h25m | Additional: 1h

NUTRITION FACTS

Calories: 164 | Carbohydrates: 29.8g | Fat: 5.2g | Protein: 1g | Cholesterol: 14mg

INGREDIENTS

- 1 (16 ounce) package large marshmallows
- 1 1/2 teaspoons green food coloring
- 1/2 cup butter, softened
- 4 1/2 cups cornflakes cereal
- 1 1/2 teaspoons vanilla extract
- 1 (2.25 ounce) package cinnamon red hot candies

DIRECTIONS

1. In a saucepan over low heat, melt together the marshmallows, butter, vanilla, and food coloring. Mix in the cornflakes cereal.
2. Drop by spoonfuls on wax paper, and decorate with red hots. Set aside, and allow to cool.

CINNAMON SUGAR COOKIES

Servings: 60 | Prep: 25m | Cooks: 15m | Total: 4h45m | Additional: 4h5m

NUTRITION FACTS

Calories: 45 | Carbohydrates: 7.4g | Fat: 1.6g | Protein: 0.4g | Cholesterol: 7mg

INGREDIENTS

- 1 1/4 cups all-purpose flour
- 3/4 cup packed light brown sugar
- 1/4 teaspoon baking soda

- 1 egg
- 1/4 teaspoon salt
- 1 teaspoon vanilla extract
- 1/2 cup butter
- 1/2 cup white sugar
- 1/4 cup white sugar
- 2 1/2 tablespoons ground cinnamon

DIRECTIONS

1. Sift together the flour, baking soda, and salt; set aside. In a medium bowl, cream butter with 1/4 cup white sugar and brown sugar. Mix in egg and vanilla. Add the sifted dry ingredients, and mix until well blended. Divide dough into 3 equal portions. Roll into logs 2 inches in diameter, wrap, and refrigerate for 3 to 4 hours. These logs can be frozen for up to 6 weeks.
2. Preheat oven to 350 degrees F (175 degrees C). Mix 1/2 cup sugar and cinnamon on a flat plate or a piece of wax paper. Unwrap dough logs, and roll in the cinnamon mixture. Cut into 1/4 inch slices, and place 2 inches apart onto ungreased cookie sheets.
3. Bake 12 to 15 minutes in the preheated oven. Remove from baking sheets to cool on wire racks. Baked cookies can be kept in an airtight container for up to 2 weeks.

PERFECT COCONUT MACAROONS

Servings: 18 | Prep: 20m | Cooks: 15m | Total: 1h20m | Additional: 45m

NUTRITION FACTS

Calories: 178 | Carbohydrates: 23.2g | Fat: 9.8g | Protein: 1.9g | Cholesterol: 0mg

INGREDIENTS

- 1 (14 ounce) package sweetened, flaked coconut
- 1/2 teaspoon almond extract
- 1/3 cup white sugar
- 1 pinch salt
- 1 tablespoon all-purpose flour
- 3 egg whites, room temperature
- 1/2 teaspoon vanilla extract
- 8 ounces semisweet chocolate chips

DIRECTIONS

1. Preheat oven to 350 degrees F (175 degrees C).
2. Line a baking sheet with parchment paper.
3. Blend coconut, sugar, flour, vanilla extract, almond extract, and salt in a food processor until combined, about 30 seconds.

4. Beat egg whites in a bowl until soft peaks form.
5. Fold coconut mixture into egg whites until just combined.
6. Wet your hands. Roll spoonfuls of coconut mixture between palms to golf ball-size cookies; arrange on the prepared baking sheet.
7. Bake cookies in the preheated oven until coconut is slightly golden and toasted, about 15 minutes. Transfer to a wire rack to cool, 30 minutes.
8. Line baking sheet with new piece of parchment paper.
9. Melt chocolate chips in the top of a double boiler over just-barely simmering water, stirring frequently and scraping down the sides with a rubber spatula to avoid scorching.
10. Dip half of each cookie in the chocolate and place on the prepared baking sheet. Place in refrigerator until chocolate is set, about 15 minutes.

CANDY CANE COOKIES

Servings: 48 | Prep: 25m | Cooks: 9m | Total: 45m | Additional: 11m

NUTRITION FACTS

Calories: 90 | Carbohydrates: 12.9g | Fat: 3.9g | Protein: 0.8g | Cholesterol: 4mg

INGREDIENTS

- 1 cup margarine
- 2 1/2 cups all-purpose flour
- 1/2 cup white sugar
- 1/2 teaspoon salt
- 1/2 cup confectioners' sugar
- 1/2 teaspoon red food coloring
- 1 egg
- 1/2 cup peppermint candy canes, crushed
- 1 teaspoon vanilla extract
- 1/2 cup white sugar for decoration
- 1/2 teaspoon peppermint extract

DIRECTIONS

1. In a large bowl, cream together the margarine, white sugar and confectioners' sugar. Beat in the egg, vanilla and peppermint extracts. Combine the flour and salt; stir into the creamed mixture until well blended. Cover or wrap dough and chill for at least one hour.
2. Preheat the oven to 375 degrees F (190 degrees C). Grease cookie sheets. Divide dough into halves. Color one half red by mixing in the food color. Roll a small amount of each dough into a 2 inch long worm. Roll them together in a twisted rope and curve the end like a cane. Place onto prepared cookie sheets.

3. Bake for 8 to 10 minutes in the preheated oven. In a small bowl, mix together the crushed candy cane and remaining white sugar. Roll hot cookies in the sugar mixture.

CHRISTMAS PINWHEEL COOKIES

Servings: 72 | Prep: 25m | Cooks: 5m | Total: 8h30m | Additional: 8h

NUTRITION FACTS

Calories: 76 | Carbohydrates: 10.2g | Fat: 3.6g | Protein: 0.9g | Cholesterol: 14mg

INGREDIENTS

- 4 cups all-purpose flour
- 2/3 cup white sugar
- 1 teaspoon baking powder
- 2 eggs, beaten
- 1/4 teaspoon baking soda
- 1 1/2 teaspoons vanilla extract
- 1 teaspoon salt
- 1 drop red food coloring, or as needed
- 1 1/3 cups butter
- 1 drop green food coloring, or as needed
- 1 cup packed brown sugar

DIRECTIONS

1. Sift the flour, baking powder, baking soda, and salt together into a bowl. Resift again into another bowl.
2. Beat the butter with the brown and white sugars in a mixing bowl until light and fluffy. Beat in the eggs and vanilla until smooth. Gradually stir in the flour mixture until evenly blended. Gather the dough into a ball, and divide into two equal parts. Place one half in a second bowl. Add red food coloring to the dough in one bowl, and green food coloring to the dough in the other bowl. Use a fork or wooden spoon to blend the food coloring into the dough until evenly blended. Add additional drops of food coloring to make the desired shade.
3. Roll out the red dough to 1/4 inch (5mm) thickness. Roll out the green dough to 1/4 inch (5mm) thickness, and place on top of the red dough. Beginning on one edge, roll the doughs to make a log so the two colors spiral inside each other. Wrap the log in waxed paper, then in a cotton towel, and refrigerate at least 8 hours.
4. Preheat oven to 400 degrees F (200 degrees C). Lightly grease 2 baking sheets.
5. Unwrap the dough log, and place on a clean, lightly floured surface. Slice the log into rounds 1/8 inch (3 mm) thick, and place on prepared baking sheets.
6. Bake in preheated oven until set, 5 to 6 minutes. Watch carefully to prevent edges from browning. Remove from oven, and cool on racks.

SCANDINAVIAN ALMOND BARS

Servings: 48 | Prep: 10m | Cooks: 10m | Total: 30m | Additional: 10m

NUTRITION FACTS

Calories: 68 | Carbohydrates: 10.5g | Fat: 2.6g | Protein: 0.9g | Cholesterol: 9mg

INGREDIENTS

- 1/2 cup butter
- 1/4 teaspoon salt
- 1 cup white sugar
- 1/2 cup sliced almonds
- 1 egg
- 2 tablespoons milk
- 1/2 teaspoon almond extract
- 1 cup confectioners' sugar
- 1 3/4 cups all-purpose flour
- 1/4 teaspoon almond extract
- 2 teaspoons baking powder
- 1/4 cup milk

DIRECTIONS

1. Preheat oven to 325 degrees F (165 degrees C).
2. In a medium bowl, cream butter and sugar. Add egg and almond extract; mix until fluffy. Stir in flour, baking powder and salt; mix well.
3. Divide dough into 4 pieces, and roll each one into a log about 12 inches long. Place 2 logs per cookie sheet 4 to 5 inches apart. Flatten each roll by hand until it is about 3 inches wide. Brush flattened roll with milk and sprinkle with sliced almonds.
4. Bake in preheated oven 12 to 15 minutes or until edges are slightly browned. While the cookies are still warm, cut them crosswise at a diagonal, into slices about 1 inch wide. When cool, drizzle with almond icing.
5. Almond icing: In a small bowl, stir together powdered sugar, almond extract, and milk until smooth. Drizzle over the cookies.

CANDY CANE COOKIES

Servings: 24 | Prep: 40m | Cooks: 20m | Total: 1h

NUTRITION FACTS

Calories: 176 | Carbohydrates: 24.2g | Fat: 8g | Protein: 1.7g | Cholesterol: 28mg

INGREDIENTS

- 1 cup butter
- 2 1/2 cups all-purpose flour
- 1 cup sifted confectioners' sugar
- 1 teaspoon salt
- 1 egg
- 1/2 cup crushed peppermint hard candies
- 1 1/2 teaspoons almond extract
- 1/2 cup white sugar
- 1 teaspoon vanilla extract

DIRECTIONS

1. Preheat oven to 375 degrees F (190 degrees C).
2. In a large bowl, combine butter, confectioners' sugar, egg, almond extract and vanilla extract. beat until smooth. Mix in flour and salt.
3. Roll into 4 inch strips, place on baking sheet. Curve top down to form handle of cane.
4. Bake in preheated oven for 9 to 10 minutes. While still warm, remove from pan and sprinkle with candy and sugar mixture.

VIENNESE CRESCENT HOLIDAY COOKIES

Servings: 48 | Prep: 15m | Cooks: 10m | Total: 1h25m | Additional: 1h

NUTRITION FACTS

Calories: 95 | Carbohydrates: 11.2g | Fat: 5.3g | Protein: 0.9g | Cholesterol: 10mg

INGREDIENTS

- 2 cups all-purpose flour
- 1/8 teaspoon salt
- 1 cup butter
- 1 teaspoon vanilla extract
- 1 cup hazelnuts, ground
- 2 cups sifted confectioners' sugar
- 1/2 cup sifted confectioners' sugar
- 1 vanilla bean

DIRECTIONS

1. Preheat oven to 375 degrees F (190 degrees C).
2. In a large mixing bowl, combine flour, butter, nuts, 1/2 cup confectioners' sugar, salt, and vanilla. Hand mix until thoroughly blended. Shape dough into a ball. Cover and refrigerate for 1 hour.

3. Meanwhile, place sugar in a bowl or small container. With sharp chef's knife, split vanilla bean lengthwise. Scrape out seeds, and mix them into the sugar. Cut pod into 2 inch pieces and mix into sugar.
4. Remove dough from refrigerator and form into 1 inch balls. Roll each ball into a small roll, 3 inches long. Place rolls 2 inches apart on ungreased cookie sheet, and bend each one to make a crescent shape.
5. Bake 10 to 12 minutes in the preheated oven, or until set but not brown.
6. Let stand 1 minute, then remove from cookie sheets. Place hot cookies on a large sheet of aluminum foil. Sprinkle with prepared sugar mixture. Turn gently to coat on both sides. Cool completely and store in an airtight container at room temperature. Just before serving, coat with more vanilla flavored sugar.

EASY TOFFEE BARS

Servings: 24 | Prep: 5m | Cooks: 15m | Total: 20m

NUTRITION FACTS

Calories: 220 | Carbohydrates: 26.1g | Fat: 13.2g | Protein: 1.8g | Cholesterol: 20mg

INGREDIENTS

- 1 cup butter
- 1 cup packed brown sugar
- 1 (10 ounce) package saltine crackers
- 1 (12 ounce) package semisweet chocolate chips

DIRECTIONS

1. Preheat oven to 400 degrees F (200 degrees C).
2. In a small saucepan over medium-high heat melt butter with brown sugar; bring to a boil and remove from heat.
3. Arrange crackers (salt side up) on a jelly roll pan. Pour butter mixture over crackers.
4. Bake in preheated oven for 5 minutes.
5. Remove from oven and sprinkle chocolate chips over crackers. Bake for another 5 minutes.

PISTACHIO CREAM CHEESE FINGERS

Servings: 100 | Prep: 30m | Cooks: 12m | Total: 1h45m | Additional: 1h3m

NUTRITION FACTS

Calories: 51 | Carbohydrates: 5.6g | Fat: 3g | Protein: 0.6g | Cholesterol: 9mg

INGREDIENTS

- 1 cup butter, softened
- 1 (3 ounce) package instant pistachio pudding mix
- 1 cup white sugar
- 1 teaspoon baking powder
- 1 (8 ounce) package cream cheese, softened
- 1/2 teaspoon salt
- 1 egg
- 3 (1 ounce) squares semisweet chocolate
- 1 teaspoon vanilla extract
- 1 teaspoon shortening
- 2 1/4 cups all-purpose flour

DIRECTIONS

1. In a large bowl, cream together the butter, sugar, and cream cheese until light and fluffy. Beat in the egg and vanilla. Combine the flour, dry pudding mix, baking powder, and salt; stir into the creamed mixture. Cover dough, and refrigerate for at least one hour for easier handling.
2. Preheat oven to 350 degrees F (175 degrees C). Grease cookie sheets. Shape teaspoonfuls of dough into finger shapes, about 1 1/2 inches long. Place cookies on prepared cookie sheets.
3. Bake for 9 to 12 minutes in the preheated oven, or until set and very lightly browned on bottoms. Cool completely on a wire rack.
4. In small saucepan over low heat, melt together chocolate and shortening, stirring constantly until smooth and well blended. Drizzle a small amount of chocolate over each cookie. Allow the chocolate to set before storing.

JAM THUMBPRINTS

Servings: 24 | Prep: 20m | Cooks: 20m | Total: 45m | Additional: 5m

NUTRITION FACTS

Calories: 126 | Carbohydrates: 12.4g | Fat: 7.9g | Protein: 1.9g | Cholesterol: 31mg

INGREDIENTS

- 2/3 cup butter
- 1 1/2 cups all-purpose flour
- 1/3 cup white sugar
- 2 egg whites, lightly beaten
- 2 egg yolks
- 3/4 cup finely chopped walnuts
- 1 teaspoon vanilla extract
- 1/3 cup strawberry preserves
- 1/2 teaspoon salt

DIRECTIONS

1. Preheat oven to 350 degrees F (175 degrees C). Lightly grease cookie sheets, or line with parchment paper.
2. In a large bowl, cream together butter and sugar until light and fluffy. Beat in egg yolks, vanilla, and salt. Gradually mix in flour.
3. Shape dough into 3/4 inch balls. Dip in lightly beaten egg whites, then roll in finely chopped walnuts. Place 1 inch apart on prepared cookie sheets. Press down center of each with thumb.
4. Bake for 15 to 17 minutes, or until golden brown. Cool on baking sheet for 5 minutes, then remove to a wire rack to cool completely. Just before serving, fill centers of cookies with strawberry preserves.

PECAN PIE COOKIES

Servings: 24 | Prep: 20m | Cooks: 10m | Total: 1h30m | Additional: 1h

NUTRITION FACTS

Calories: 185 | Carbohydrates: 22.1g | Fat: 10.4g | Protein: 1.7g | Cholesterol: 28mg

INGREDIENTS

- 1/4 cup butter
- 1 teaspoon baking powder
- 1/2 cup confectioners' sugar
- 1 cup brown sugar, packed
- 3 tablespoons light corn syrup
- 3/4 cup butter, softened
- 3/4 cup finely chopped pecans
- 1 egg
- 2 cups all-purpose flour
- 1 teaspoon vanilla extract

DIRECTIONS

1. Melt 1/4 cup of butter in a saucepan, and stir in the confectioners' sugar and corn syrup until the sugar is dissolved. Bring to a boil over medium heat, stirring often, and stir in the pecans until well combined. Refrigerate the mixture for 30 minutes to chill.
2. Preheat oven to 350 degrees F (175 degrees C). Sift the flour and baking powder together in a bowl, and set aside.
3. Beat brown sugar, 3/4 cup butter, egg, and vanilla extract in a large bowl with an electric mixer on medium speed until the mixture is creamy, about 2 minutes. Gradually beat in the flour mixture until well mixed. Pinch off about 1 tablespoon of dough, and roll it into a ball. Press the dough into the bottom of an ungreased cupcake pan cup, and use your thumb to press the dough into a small

piecrust shape, with 1/4-inch walls up the sides of the cupcake cup. Repeat with the rest of the dough. Fill each little crust with about 1 teaspoon of the prepared pecan filling.

4. Bake in the preheated oven until the cookie shells are lightly browned, 10 to 13 minutes. Watch closely after 10 minutes. Let the cookies cool in the cupcake pans for 5 minutes before removing to wire rack to finish cooling.

ROSETTES

Servings: 30 | Prep: 15m | Cooks: 1h30m | Total: 1h45m

NUTRITION FACTS

Calories: 561 | Carbohydrates: 8.2g | Fat: 59.2g | Protein: 1.1g | Cholesterol: 13mg

INGREDIENTS

- 2 eggs
- 1 teaspoon vanilla extract
- 1 tablespoon white sugar
- 1/4 teaspoon salt
- 1 cup sifted all-purpose flour
- vegetable oil for frying
- 1 cup milk
- sifted confectioners' sugar

DIRECTIONS

1. Combine eggs, sugar and salt; beat well. Add remaining ingredients and beat until smooth.
2. Heat a rosette iron in deep, hot oil (375 degrees) for 2 minutes.
3. Drain excess oil from iron. Dip in batter to 1/4 inch from the top of the iron, then dip iron immediately into hot oil (375 degrees).
4. Fry rosette until golden, about 30 seconds. Lift out; tip upside down to drain. With fork, push rosette off iron onto a rack placed over paper towels.
5. Reheat iron 1 minute; make next rosette.
6. Sprinkle rosettes with confectioners' sugar.

BUTTERSCOTCH DROPS

Servings: 24 | Prep: 10m | Cooks: 5m | Total: 1h15m | Additional: 1h

NUTRITION FACTS

Calories: 152 | Carbohydrates: 14.3g | Fat: 9.1g | Protein: 3g | Cholesterol: 0mg

INGREDIENTS

- 1 (11 ounce) package butterscotch chips
- 1 cup creamy peanut butter
- 4 cups cornflakes cereal

DIRECTIONS

1. In a medium saucepan over medium heat, melt butterscotch chips and peanut butter together. Remove from stove and stir in cornflakes. Drop by spoonfuls onto cookie sheets. Chill to harden.

LINDA'S CRANBERRY COOKIES

Servings: 36 | Prep: 20m | Cooks: 10m | Total: 1h | Additional: 30m

NUTRITION FACTS

Calories: 139 | Carbohydrates: 17.5g | Fat: 7.1g | Protein: 1.5g | Cholesterol: 25mg

INGREDIENTS

- 2 1/4 cups all-purpose flour
- 1 (3.5 ounce) package instant vanilla pudding mix
- 1 teaspoon baking soda
- 1 teaspoon vanilla extract
- 1 cup butter
- 2 eggs
- 1/4 cup white sugar
- 1 (6 ounce) package white chocolate chips
- 3/4 cup brown sugar
- 1/2 (6 ounce) package dried cranberries

DIRECTIONS

1. Preheat an oven to 350 degrees F (175 degrees C). Lightly grease two baking sheets. Combine flour and baking soda in a bowl.
2. Beat the butter, white sugar, brown sugar, and instant pudding with an electric mixer in a large bowl until smooth. Beat the first egg into the butter until completely blended, then beat in the vanilla with the last egg. Mix in the flour mixture until just incorporated. Fold in the white chocolate chips and cranberries; mixing just enough to evenly combine. Drop spoonfuls of the dough 2 inches apart onto prepared baking sheets.
3. Bake in the preheated oven until edges of the cookies become golden brown, 9 to 12 minutes. Cool in the baking sheet for 10 minutes before removing to cool completely on a wire rack.

COOKIE MIX IN A JAR

Servings: 36 | Prep: 20m | Cooks: 0m | Total: 20m

Calories: 67 | Carbohydrates: 15.4g | Fat: 0.4g | Protein: 1.1g | Cholesterol: 0mg

INGREDIENTS

- 1 cup all-purpose flour
- 3/4 cup raisins
- 1 teaspoon ground cinnamon
- 2 cups rolled oats
- 1/2 teaspoon ground nutmeg
- 3/4 cup packed brown sugar
- 1 teaspoon baking soda
- 1/2 cup white sugar
- 1/2 teaspoon salt

DIRECTIONS

1. Mix together flour, ground cinnamon, ground nutmeg, baking soda, and salt. Set aside.
2. Layer ingredients in the following order into a 1 quart, wide mouth canning jar: Flour mixture, raisins, rolled oats, brown sugar, and white sugar. It will be a tight fit, make sure you firmly pack down each layer before adding the next layer.
3. Attach a tag with the following instructions: Oatmeal Raisin Spice Cookies 1. Preheat oven to 350 degrees F (175 degrees C). Line cookie sheets with parchment paper. 2. Empty jar of cookie mix into large mixing bowl. Use your hands to thoroughly mix. 3. Mix in 3/4 cup butter or margarine, softened. Stir in one slightly beaten egg and 1 teaspoon of vanilla. Mix until completely blended. You will need to finish mixing with your hands. Shape into balls the size of walnuts. Place on a parchment lined cookie sheets 2 inches apart. 4. Bake for 11 to 13 minutes in preheated oven, or until edges are lightly browned. Cool 5 minutes on cookie sheet. Transfer cookies to wire racks to finish cooling.

VENICE HIGH SCHOOL CHERRY BUTTER COOKIES

Servings: 42 | Prep: 15m | Cooks: 15m | Total: 30m

NUTRITION FACTS

Calories: 160 | Carbohydrates: 17g | Fat: 9.7g | Protein: 1.7g | Cholesterol: 23mg

INGREDIENTS

- 2 cups butter, softened
- 4 1/2 cups sifted all-purpose flour
- 2 teaspoons vanilla extract
- 1/2 cup chopped walnuts

* 2 cups confectioners' sugar
* 1/2 cup chopped maraschino cherries
* 1/4 teaspoon salt

DIRECTIONS

1. Preheat the oven to 350 degrees F (175 degrees C).
2. In a large bowl, mix together the butter, vanilla and confectioners' sugar until smooth. Mix in salt, then stir in flour by hand until dough is stiff. Add the walnuts and cherries, and mix into the dough, kneading like bread on a clean floured surface.
3. Roll dough into ping pong sized balls, and place onto ungreased cookie sheets. Press down balls with a fork to make a criss cross pattern on top.
4. Bake for 15 to 17 minutes in the preheated oven. Let stand on the baking sheet for a few minutes before removing to wire racks to cool completely.

CHRISTMAS STARS

Servings: 24 | Prep: 30m | Cooks: 15m | Total: 4h45m | Additional: 4h

NUTRITION FACTS

Calories: 158 | Carbohydrates: 23.7g | Fat: 6.3g | Protein: 1.9g | Cholesterol: 31mg

INGREDIENTS

* 3/4 cup butter, softened
* 1 teaspoon baking powder
* 1 cup white sugar
* 1/4 teaspoon salt
* 2 egg
* 6 tablespoons strawberry jam
* 1 teaspoon vanilla extract
* 1/4 cup green decorator sugar (optional)
* 2 1/2 cups all-purpose flour

DIRECTIONS

1. In a large bowl, cream butter and sugar until light and fluffy. Gradually add eggs and vanilla. Mix well. Sift together flour, baking powder, and salt. Stir flour mixture into the butter mixture until well blended. Divide dough in half and wrap in plastic. Refrigerate dough for three hours.
2. Preheat oven to 350 degrees F (175 degrees C). Grease two cookie sheets or line them with parchment paper.
3. On a floured surface, roll out half of the dough to 1/8 inch thickness. Cut dough into star shapes using a 3- to 4-inch star cookie cutter. Using a 1- to 2-inch star cookie cutter, cut a star into the

center of half of the big stars. Place the full stars on one cookie sheet and the "tops"--the cookies with the center cutouts--on another. Sprinkle colored sugar on the star tops, if desired.

4. Bake in preheated oven until edges are golden brown, 6 to 8 minutes. Allow cookies to cool completely. (You can re-roll the mini stars cut out of the centers, or bake them separately for about 5 minutes.) Repeat with remaining cookie dough.

5. After cookies cool completely, spread 1 teaspoon of preserves in the center of each full star cookie. Place a cut-out cookie on top of the layer of preserves. Pack cookies between waxed paper in a covered tin to preserve freshness.

LIGHTER SNICKERDOODLES

Servings: 24 | Prep: 20m | Cooks: 10m | Total: 1h50m | Additional: 1h20m

NUTRITION FACTS

Calories: 142 | Carbohydrates: 26.2g | Fat: 3.1g | Protein: 2.6g | Cholesterol: 15mg

INGREDIENTS

- 1/4 cup butter
- 2 teaspoons cream of tartar
- 1 1/2 cups white sugar
- 1 teaspoon baking soda
- 4 ounces lowfat cream cheese
- 1/4 teaspoon salt
- 1 egg
- 1/4 cup white sugar
- 2 egg whites
- 2 teaspoons ground cinnamon
- 2 3/4 cups all-purpose flour

DIRECTIONS

1. In a large bowl, cream together the butter, 1 1/2 cups of white sugar, and cream cheese. Beat in the egg and egg whites until smooth. Sift together the flour, cream of tartar, baking soda, and salt; stir into the creamed mixture. Cover, and refrigerate dough for at least 1 hour.

2. Preheat oven to 400 degrees F (200 degrees C). In a small dish, mix together the remaining white sugar and the cinnamon. Roll the dough into walnut sized balls, and roll the balls in the cinnamon and sugar mixture. Place the balls at least 2 inches apart on cookie sheets, and flatten slightly.

3. Bake for 8 to 10 minutes in the preheated oven. Remove from cookie sheets to cool on wire racks.

NUTELLA HAZELNUT COOKIES

Servings: 12 | Prep: 30m | Cooks: 12m | Total: 57m | Additional: 15m

Calories: 502 | Carbohydrates: 63.1g | Fat: 26.7g | Protein: 6.1g | Cholesterol: 68mg

INGREDIENTS

- 2 1/2 cups all-purpose flour
- 3/4 cup white sugar
- 1/4 cup unsweetened cocoa powder
- 2 large eggs
- 1 teaspoon baking soda
- 2 tablespoons vanilla extract
- 1 teaspoon salt
- 1/2 cup chocolate-hazelnut spread, such as Nutella
- 1 cup butter, room temperature
- 1/2 cup chopped toasted hazelnuts
- 3/4 cup brown sugar
- 1 cup chocolate chips

DIRECTIONS

1. Preheat oven to 350 degrees F (175 degrees C). Grease a baking sheet or line it with parchment paper.
2. Combine flour, cocoa powder, baking soda, and salt in a bowl. Mix with a whisk to break up any lumps.
3. Beat butter, brown sugar, and white sugar with an electric mixer in a large bowl until smooth. Beat in eggs one at a time until completely incorporated. Mix in vanilla and chocolate-hazelnut spread.
4. Slowly add in flour mixture and stir just until combined. Fold in chopped hazelnuts and chocolate chips. Drop the dough onto prepared baking sheet by tablespoons or with a cookie scoop.
5. Bake in preheated oven until edges look dry and cookies are fragrant, about 12 minutes. Allow to cool for 1 minute on baking sheet before transferring to a wire rack.

CHOCOLATE ORANGE COOKIES

Servings: 36 | Prep: 30m | Cooks: 10m | Total: 50m | Additional: 10m

NUTRITION FACTS

Calories: 75 | Carbohydrates: 8.5g | Fat: 4.4g | Protein: 0.9g | Cholesterol: 15mg

INGREDIENTS

- 1 (1 ounce) square unsweetened chocolate
- 1 1/2 cups all-purpose flour
- 3/4 cup butter

- 1 teaspoon baking powder
- 3/4 cup white sugar
- 1 pinch salt
- 1 egg
- 1 tablespoon orange zest
- 1 teaspoon vanilla extract

DIRECTIONS

1. Preheat the oven to 350 degrees F (175 degrees C). In a microwave-safe dish, melt the unsweetened chocolate, stirring frequently until smooth. Set aside.
2. In a medium bowl, cream together the butter and sugar until smooth. Beat in the egg and vanilla. Combine the flour, baking powder, and salt; stir into the creamed mixture. Divide dough in two. Mix orange zest into one half, and melted chocolate into the other half. Use a bit of each mixture to form a ball about 1 inch in diameter.
3. Bake for 8 to 10 minutes in the preheated oven, or until center is set. Cool on wire racks.

SNOWBALLS

Servings: 24 | Prep: 15m | Cooks: 25m | Total: 55m | Additional: 15m

NUTRITION FACTS

Calories: 170 | Carbohydrates: 16.7g | Fat: 11g | Protein: 1.6g | Cholesterol: 20mg

INGREDIENTS

- 1 cup butter
- 3/4 teaspoon salt
- 1/2 cup white sugar
- 1 cup chopped pecans
- 1 tablespoon vanilla extract
- 3/4 cup sifted confectioners' sugar
- 2 cups sifted all-purpose flour

DIRECTIONS

1. Preheat oven to 325 degrees F (165 degrees C.) Lightly butter 2 baking sheets, or line with parchment paper.
2. Cream the butter, sugar, and vanilla until light and fluffy. Sift together the flour and salt; mix into the butter mixture. Stir in the pecans. Dust your hands with a little of the confectioners' sugar and roll the dough into 1 inch balls.
3. Place 2 inches apart on the baking sheets and bake for 25 minutes or just until brown. Put on racks to cool for 15 minutes, then roll in the confectioners sugar.

SPUMONI CHOCOLATE CHIP COOKIES

Servings: 24 | Prep: 20m | Cooks: 10m | Total: 30m

NUTRITION FACTS

Calories: 247 | Carbohydrates: 32.2g | Fat: 13.1g | Protein: 2.7g | Cholesterol: 36mg

INGREDIENTS

* 2 1/4 cups all-purpose flour
* 2 eggs
* 1 teaspoon baking soda
* 1 teaspoon vanilla extract
* 1 cup butter, softened
* 1 (12 ounce) bag semi-sweet chocolate chips
* 1/4 cup white sugar
* 1/2 cup chopped maraschino cherries
* 3/4 cup packed brown sugar
* 1/4 cup chopped pistachios
* 1 (3.4 ounce) package instant pistachio pudding mix

DIRECTIONS

1. Preheat oven to 350 degrees F (175 degrees C). Sift together the flour and baking soda; set aside.
2. Cream together the butter, white sugar, and brown sugar in a large bowl until smooth. Stir in the instant pudding mix until well combined. Beat in the eggs one at a time, then stir in the vanilla. Blend in the flour mixture. Fold in the chocolate chips, cherries, and pistachios. Drop by large spoonfuls onto ungreased baking pans.
3. Bake in the preheated oven until light brown, about 10 minutes.

GREAT GRANDAD'S SUGAR COOKIES

Servings: 30 | Prep: 30m | Cooks: 10m | Total: 1h10m | Additional: 30m

NUTRITION FACTS

Calories: 258 | Carbohydrates: 36.4g | Fat: 11.1g | Protein: 3.5g | Cholesterol: 19mg

INGREDIENTS

* 6 cups all-purpose flour
* 1 1/2 cups shortening
* 1 tablespoon baking powder
* 1 teaspoon baking soda
* 1 teaspoon ground nutmeg

- 1 cup sour milk
- 1 pinch salt
- 3 eggs, beaten
- 2 1/2 cups white sugar
- 1 teaspoon vanilla extract

DIRECTIONS

1. Preheat oven to 350 degrees F (175 degrees C). Line cookie sheets with parchment paper.
2. In a medium bowl, stir together 4 cups flour, baking powder, nutmeg, salt, and sugar. Cut in the shortening until the mixture resembles coarse crumbs. Stir in baking soda, sour milk, beaten eggs, and vanilla. Stir as little as possible, and add the remaining flour as necessary to make dough thick enough to roll out.
3. On a lightly floured surface, roll out dough 1/4 inch thick. Cut into desired shapes with cookie cutters. Place cookies 1 inch apart on the prepared cookie sheets.
4. Bake for 8 to 10 minutes in preheated oven. Cool on baking sheets.

COUNTRY OATMEAL COOKIE IN A JAR
Servings: 12 | Prep: 15m | Cooks: 15m | Total: 30m

NUTRITION FACTS

Calories: 314 | Carbohydrates: 52.8g | Fat: 11.2g | Protein: 4.6g | Cholesterol: 0mg

INGREDIENTS

- 3/4 cup white sugar
- 1 1/2 teaspoons baking powder
- 3/4 cup packed brown sugar
- 1/2 teaspoon salt
- 1 cup rolled oats
- 1 cup semisweet chocolate chips
- 1 1/2 cups all-purpose flour
- 1 cup chopped walnuts (optional)

DIRECTIONS

1. Using a 1 quart or 1 liter jar, layer in the ingredients in the order given. Pack down the jar after each addition. Put the lid on, and cover with an 8 inch circle of fabric. Secure the fabric over the lid using a rubber band, then cover the rubber band by tying a nice piece of ribbon or raffia around the lid. Attach a tag to the ribbon with the following instructions.
2. Preheat oven to 350 degrees F (175 degrees C). In a medium bowl, cream together 3/4 cup of softened butter, with 2 eggs and 1 teaspoon of vanilla. Add the entire contents of the jar, and mix by

hand until combined. Drop dough by heaping spoonfuls onto an unprepared cookie sheet. Bake for 12 to 15 minutes in the preheated oven.

PEPPERMINT MERINGUE COOKIES

Servings: 56 | Prep: 15m | Cooks: 1h30m | Total: 1h45m

NUTRITION FACTS

Calories: 11 | Carbohydrates: 2.7g | Fat: 0g | Protein: 0.1g | Cholesterol: 0mg

INGREDIENTS

- 2 egg whites
- 1/3 cup white sugar
- 1/8 teaspoon cider vinegar
- 3 peppermint candy canes, crushed
- 1/8 teaspoon salt

DIRECTIONS

1. Preheat the oven to 225 degrees F (110 degrees C). Line cookie sheets with aluminum foil or parchment paper.
2. In a large glass or metal bowl, whip egg whites, vinegar and salt to soft peaks. Gradually add sugar while continuing to whip until stiff peaks form, about 5 minutes. Fold in 1/3 of the crushed candy canes, reserving the rest. Drop by heaping teaspoonfuls, one inch apart onto the prepared cookie sheets. Sprinkle remaining crushed candy canes over the top.
3. Bake for 90 minutes in the preheated oven, or until dry. Cool on baking sheets.

CHEF JOHN'S RUSSIAN TEA CAKES

Servings: 14 | Prep: 15m | Cooks: 15m | Total: 30m

NUTRITION FACTS

Calories: 321 | Carbohydrates: 36.1g | Fat: 18.8g | Protein: 3.4g | Cholesterol: 35mg

INGREDIENTS

- 1 cup unsalted butter, room temperature
- 1 teaspoon vanilla extract
- 1 1/3 cups confectioners' sugar, divided
- 2 cups all-purpose flour
- 1 cup finely chopped toasted walnuts
- 2 tablespoons all-purpose flour

- 1/8 teaspoon salt
- 1 cup confectioners' sugar for dusting, or more as needed

DIRECTIONS

1. Preheat oven to 350 degrees F (175 degrees C). Arrange rack in center position of oven.
2. Place butter, 1/3 cup packed powdered sugar, walnuts, salt, and vanilla in a bowl. Top with the flour. Mix with your clean hands until the dough starts to clump up. Keep mixing by hand until all the flour and clumps of butter are evenly mixed into the dough and it can be easily formed into balls.
3. Scoop out dough and roll by hand into uniformly round balls, just slightly larger than 1 inch. Place on a rimmed baking sheet lined with a silicone baking mat about 2 inches apart.
4. Bake in preheated oven until lightly golden, 15 to 25 minutes depending on the size of the cookies.
5. Let cool exactly 5 minutes then roll in remaining 1 cup confectioners' sugar. Let cookies cool completely and toss them again in the confectioners' sugar.

CHEWY WHITE CHOCOLATE CHIP GINGERBREAD COOKIES

Servings: 24 | Prep: 20m | Cooks: 10m | Total: 1h30m | Additional: 1h

NUTRITION FACTS

Calories: 231 | Carbohydrates: 31.2g | Fat: 11.1g | Protein: 2.4g | Cholesterol: 26mg

INGREDIENTS

- 3/4 cup butter
- 1 teaspoon ground cinnamon
- 1 cup white sugar
- 1/2 teaspoon ground cloves
- 1 beaten egg
- 1/2 teaspoon nutmeg
- 1/4 cup molasses
- 1/2 teaspoon salt
- 2 cups all-purpose flour
- 1 (12 ounce) package white chocolate chips
- 2 teaspoons baking soda
- 1/2 cup white sugar, for rolling
- 1 teaspoon ground ginger

DIRECTIONS

1. Beat together the butter with 1 cup of sugar in a mixing bowl until the mixture is smooth, and stir in beaten egg and molasses. In another bowl, whisk together the flour, baking soda, ginger, cinnamon,

cloves, nutmeg, and salt; stir the flour mixture into the molasses mixture by half cupfuls. Stir in the white chocolate chips. Refrigerate dough for at least 1 hour.

2. Preheat oven to 350 degrees F (175 degrees C).

3. Scoop up a generous spoonful of dough, and roll it into a ball. Roll the ball in sugar, place onto an ungreased baking sheet, and flatten slightly. Sprinkle a little sugar onto the cookie, if desired. Repeat for the rest of the cookies.

4. Bake the cookies in the preheated oven until lightly browned, 10 to 15 minutes. Allow to cool on the baking sheet for about 1 minute before removing to finish cooling on racks.

BETZ'S GOOD SUGAR COOKIES

Servings: 48 | Prep: 20m | Cooks: 10m | Total: 9h | Additional: 8h30m

NUTRITION FACTS

Calories: 81 | Carbohydrates: 10.3g | Fat: 4.1g | Protein: 0.8g | Cholesterol: 18mg

INGREDIENTS

- 1 cup butter
- 1 teaspoon lemon extract
- 1 1/2 cups white sugar
- 2 cups all-purpose flour
- 2 eggs
- 1 teaspoon baking powder
- 1 teaspoon vanilla extract
- 1 pinch salt

DIRECTIONS

1. In a large bowl, cream together the butter and sugar until fluffy. Beat in the eggs one at a time, then stir in the vanilla and lemon extracts. Combine the flour, baking powder, and salt; gradually blend into the creamed mixture to form a soft dough. Cover or wrap dough, and refrigerate overnight.

2. Preheat the oven to 400 degrees F (200 degrees C). On a floured surface, roll the dough out 1/4 inch thick. Cut into desired shapes using cookie cutters. Place cookies 2 inches apart on ungreased cookie sheets.

3. Bake for 10 minutes in the preheated oven, or until lightly browned. Cool on wire racks.

TINY TARTS

Servings: 12 | Prep: 30m | Cooks: 30m | Total: 2h | Additional: 1h

NUTRITION FACTS

Calories: 228 | Carbohydrates: 22.3g | Fat: 14.8g | Protein: 2.7g | Cholesterol: 22.3mg

INGREDIENTS

- 1/2 cup butter, softened
- 3/4 cup packed brown sugar
- 1 (3 ounce) package cream cheese, softened
- 1 tablespoon margarine, melted
- 1 cup all-purpose flour
- 1/2 cup chopped pecans
- 1 egg

DIRECTIONS

1. Preheat the oven toe 325 degrees F (165 degrees C).
2. Beat softened margarine or butter and cream cheese until thoroughly combined. Stir in flour.
3. Using 24 ungreased 1 3/4 inch mini muffin cups, press a rounded teaspoon of pastry evenly into the bottom and up the sides of each cup.
4. To Make The Filling: Beat the egg and mix in the brown sugar, melted margarine or butter and the chopped pecans.
5. Fill each pastry-lined muffin cup with about 1 heaping teaspoon of pecan filling. Bake at 325 degrees F (165 degrees C) for about 30 minutes or until pastry is golden and filling is puffed. Cool slightly in the muffin cups, then remove and cool completely on a wire rack.

MY FAVORITE SUGAR COOKIES

Servings: 12 | Prep: 30m | Cooks: 8m | Total: 2h38m | Additional: 2h

NUTRITION FACTS

Calories: 337 | Carbohydrates: 51.3g | Fat: 12.6g | Protein: 4.9g | Cholesterol: 31mg

INGREDIENTS

- 1 1/2 cups white sugar
- 3 1/4 cups all-purpose flour
- 2/3 cup shortening
- 2 1/2 teaspoons baking powder
- 2 eggs
- 1/2 teaspoon salt
- 2 tablespoons milk
- 1 egg white (optional)
- 1 teaspoon vanilla extract

DIRECTIONS

1. Combine sugar and shortening in a mixing bowl. Beat at low speed just until smooth. Mix in eggs, milk, and vanilla.
2. In separate bowl, whisk flour, baking soda and salt. Pour into sugar mixture and blend until combined.
3. Shape dough into a ball and wrap with waxed paper or plastic wrap. Refrigerate 2 to 3 hours until easy to handle.
4. Preheat oven to 400 degrees F (200 degrees C). Lightly grease cookie sheets or line them with parchment paper.
5. Roll out half of the dough at a time on a lightly floured surface. Keep the remaining dough refrigerated. For crisp cookies, roll paper-thin. For softer cookies, roll 1/8 to 1/4 inch thick.
6. With floured cookie cutters, cut dough into various shapes. Re-roll dough trimmings into a ball, cover and refrigerate, and continue to cut shapes with chilled dough.
7. Place cookies 1/2 inch apart on greased cookie sheets. To glaze, brush tops of cookies with heavy or whipping cream or with an egg white slightly beaten with 1 tablespoon of water.
8. Sprinkle cookies with your choice of toppings; bake 8 minutes or until very light brown. Remove cookies and cool completely.

SUPER DUPER CHOCOLATE COOKIES

Servings: 48 | Prep: 20m | Cooks: 15m | Total: 3h35m | Additional: 3h

NUTRITION FACTS

Calories: 104 | Carbohydrates: 15.2g | Fat: 4.6g | Protein: 1.6g | Cholesterol: 16mg

INGREDIENTS

- 4 (1 ounce) squares unsweetened chocolate
- 1/2 cup vegetable shortening
- 2 cups white sugar
- 2 teaspoons vanilla extract
- 4 eggs
- 2 cups all-purpose flour
- 2 teaspoons baking powder
- 1/8 teaspoon salt
- 1/2 cup chopped walnuts
- 3/4 cup confectioners' sugar

DIRECTIONS

1. Melt the chocolate and shortening in a saucepan over low heat. Remove from heat and mix in sugar and vanilla. Beat in eggs 1 at a time. In a bowl, sift together flour, baking powder and salt. Stir in the chocolate mixture and nuts. Chill dough in the refrigerator 3 hours or overnight.
2. Preheat oven to 350 degrees F (175 degrees C). Grease cookie sheets.

3. Place confectioners' sugar in a bowl. Roll dough into 1 inch balls. Roll dough balls in confectioners' sugar to coat. Arrange 3 inches apart on the prepared cookie sheets.
4. Bake 12 to 15 minutes in the preheated oven. The cookies will look soft when removed from the oven. Transfer to a wire rack to cool. Enjoy.

BROWN SUGAR COOKIES

Servings: 60 | Prep: 10m | Cooks: 10m | Total: 50m | Additional: 30m

NUTRITION FACTS

Calories: 62 | Carbohydrates: 10.8g | Fat: 1.8g | Protein: 0.8g | Cholesterol: 10mg

INGREDIENTS

- 2 cups brown sugar
- 2 1/2 cups all-purpose flour
- 1/2 cup unsalted butter, softened
- 3/4 teaspoon baking powder
- 2 large eggs
- 1/2 teaspoon salt
- 1 teaspoon vanilla extract
- 1 cup confectioners' sugar

DIRECTIONS

1. Preheat oven to 350 degrees F (175 degrees C).
2. Beat brown sugar, butter, eggs, and vanilla extract together in a bowl using an electric mixer until smooth and creamy.
3. Whisk flour, baking powder, and salt together in a separate bowl. Stir flour mixture into butter mixture until dough is fully combined.
4. Pour confectioners' sugar onto a large plate. Spoon dough, 1 1/2 teaspoons per cookie, onto confectioners' sugar and roll to coat. Arrange coated dough on a baking sheet.
5. Bake in the preheated oven until edges are lightly browned, 12 to 14 minutes. Cool cookies on baking pan for 2 minutes before transferring to a wire rack to cool completely.

APPLESAUCE COOKIES

Servings: 60 | Prep: 15m | Cooks: 12m | Total: 51m | Additional: 24m

NUTRITION FACTS

Calories: 78 | Carbohydrates: 10.5g | Fat: 3.8g | Protein: 1g | Cholesterol: 3mg

INGREDIENTS

- 1 cup packed brown sugar
- 1/2 teaspoon salt
- 1 egg
- 3/4 teaspoon ground cinnamon
- 3/4 cup shortening
- 1/4 teaspoon ground nutmeg
- 1 cup applesauce
- 1/4 teaspoon ground cloves
- 2 1/2 cups all-purpose flour
- 1 cup chopped walnuts
- 1/2 teaspoon baking soda
- 1 cup raisins

DIRECTIONS

1. Preheat the oven to 325 degrees F (165 degrees C). Grease cookie sheets.
2. In a medium bowl, cream together the brown sugar and shortening until smooth. Stir in the egg, and then the applesauce until well blended. Combine the flour, baking soda, salt, cinnamon, nutmeg, and cloves; stir into the applesauce mixture. Mix in walnuts and raisins. Drop by teaspoonfuls onto the prepared cookie sheets.
3. Bake for 10 to 12 minutes in the preheated oven, until the edges start to brown. Cool on cookie sheets for a few minutes before removing to wire racks to cool completely.

CHERRY POPPYSEED TWINKS

Servings: 30 | Prep: 25m | Cooks: 15m | Total: 1h | Additional: 20m

NUTRITION FACTS

Calories: 121 | Carbohydrates: 14.5g | Fat: 6.6g | Protein: 1.3g | Cholesterol: 22mg

INGREDIENTS

- 1 cup butter, softened
- 2 cups all-purpose flour
- 1 cup confectioners' sugar
- 1/2 teaspoon salt
- 1 egg
- 2 tablespoons poppy seeds
- 1 teaspoon vanilla extract
- 1/2 cup cherry preserves

DIRECTIONS

1. Preheat oven to 300 degrees F (150 degrees C).

2. Cream together butter and confectioners' sugar until light and fluffy. Beat in egg and vanilla. Mix in flour, salt, and poppy seeds until well blended. Drop dough from a teaspoon onto an ungreased cookie sheet. Make an indention in the middle of each cookie with your finger. If the dough is too sticky, dip your finger in water first. Fill each hole with about 1/2 teaspoon of cherry preserves.
3. Bake in preheated oven for 20 to 25 minutes, or until edges begin to brown.

GINGERBREAD MAN COOKIES

Servings: 48 | Prep: 30m | Cooks: 10m | Total: 1d | Additional: 1d

NUTRITION FACTS

Calories: 84 | Carbohydrates: 14.8g | Fat: 2.3g | Protein: 1.1g | Cholesterol: 4mg

INGREDIENTS

- 3 1/2 cups all-purpose flour
- 1 egg
- 1 1/2 teaspoons ground ginger
- 1 cup molasses
- 1 1/2 teaspoons ground cinnamon
- 1 teaspoon baking soda
- 1/4 teaspoon salt
- 1 1/2 teaspoons warm water
- 1/2 cup shortening
- 1/4 cup raisins for decorating
- 1/2 cup white sugar

DIRECTIONS

1. Combine flour, ginger, cinnamon, and salt in a bowl and set aside.
2. In large bowl, cream shortening and sugar until smooth. Mix in egg and molasses. Dissolve baking soda in 1 1/2 teaspoons warm water and add to egg mixture; stir until combined.
3. Mix in dry ingredients well blended. Shape dough into a disk, wrap in plastic, and refrigerate overnight.
4. Preheat oven to 350 degrees F. Grease cookie sheets or line them with parchment paper.
5. Lightly flour a work surface. Roll out dough to a thickness of 1/4 inch. Cut out gingerbread men using cookie cutters and place 2 inches apart on cookie sheets. Use raisins to make eyes, noses and buttons.
6. Bake in the preheated oven, or until firm, 10 to 12 minutes. Let cool on wire racks.

EMILY'S FAMOUS CHOCOLATE SHORTBREAD COOKIES

Servings: 60 | Prep: 20m | Cooks: 10m | Total: 30m

NUTRITION FACTS

Calories: 101 | Carbohydrates: 11.6g | Fat: 5.8g | Protein: 1.3g | Cholesterol: 18mg

INGREDIENTS

- 2 cups confectioners' sugar
- 1 1/2 cups unsalted butter, chilled and cubed
- 1/2 cup Dutch process cocoa powder
- 1 teaspoon vanilla extract
- 3 1/2 cups all-purpose flour
- 2 eggs
- 1/2 teaspoon salt
- 1 cup chopped semisweet chocolate

DIRECTIONS

1. Preheat oven to 350 degrees F (175 degrees C).
2. In a large bowl, stir together the confectioners' sugar, cocoa, flour and salt until well blended. Cut in the butter until lumps are no larger than peas. Add eggs and vanilla; mix until a stiff dough forms. It may take a minute to come together.
3. On a lightly floured surface, roll out dough to 1/4 inch thickness and cut into desired shapes using cookie cutters. If the dough is too sticky, chill for a little bit. Place cookies 2 inches apart onto an ungreased baking sheet.
4. Bake for 8 to 10 minutes in the preheated oven, or until the surface appears dry. Allow cookies to cool for a couple minutes on the baking sheet before removing to wire racks to cool completely. When cookies are completely cool, melt the chocolate over a double boiler or in the microwave. Stir frequently until smooth. Dip cookies or drizzle with the chocolate and place on waxed paper to set.

DEVIL'S FOOD PEANUT BUTTER CHIP COOKIES

Servings: 30 | Prep: 10m | Cooks: 12m | Total: 45m | Additional: 23m

NUTRITION FACTS

Calories: 211 | Carbohydrates: 20.1g | Fat: 11.8g | Protein: 5.2g | Cholesterol: 16mg

INGREDIENTS

- 2 eggs
- 1 (18.25 ounce) package devil's food cake mix
- 1 teaspoon vanilla extract
- 2 cups peanut butter chips
- 2/3 cup shortening

DIRECTIONS

1. Preheat oven to 375 degrees F (190 degrees C).
2. In a medium bowl, beat the eggs, vanilla, and shortening with 1/2 of the cake mix until light and fluffy. Mix in the remaining cake mix and the peanut butter chips. Drop dough by rounded teaspoonfuls 2 inches apart onto ungreased cookie sheets.
3. Bake for 10 to 12 minutes in preheated oven. Remove from cookie sheets to cool on wire racks.

PECAN FILLED COOKIES

Servings: 30 | Prep: 15m | Cooks: 8m | Total: 45m | Additional: 22m

NUTRITION FACTS

Calories: 98 | Carbohydrates: 12.6g | Fat: 4.8g | Protein: 1.3g | Cholesterol: 15mg

INGREDIENTS

- 1/2 cup butter
- 1/2 teaspoon baking soda
- 1 cup light brown sugar
- 1/4 teaspoon salt
- 1 egg
- 1/2 cup chopped pecans
- 1 teaspoon vanilla extract
- 1/8 cup sour cream
- 2 cups all-purpose flour
- 1/4 cup brown sugar

DIRECTIONS

1. Preheat oven to 350 degrees F (175 degrees C). Grease cookie sheets.
2. In a medium bowl, cream together the butter and 1 cup brown sugar until smooth. Beat in the egg and stir in the vanilla. Combine the flour, baking soda and salt; stir into the sugar mixture. Roll the dough into 1 inch balls and place them 2 inches apart onto the prepared cookie sheets. Make a depression in the center using the cap from the vanilla or the end of a wooden spoon. Mix together the pecans, sour cream and 1/4 cup brown sugar; fill each depression with the mixture.
3. Bake for 8 to 11 minutes in the preheated oven, or until light brown. Cool for a few minutes on the cookie sheets before removing to wire racks to cool completely.

HAMANTASHEN

Servings: 36 | Prep: 2h | Cooks: 15m | Total: 2h15m

NUTRITION FACTS

Calories: 184 | Carbohydrates: 23.4g | Fat: 8.9g | Protein: 2.5g | Cholesterol: 31mg

INGREDIENTS

- 1 1/2 cups butter or margarine, softened
- 1 tablespoon vanilla extract
- 1 cup white sugar
- 2 teaspoons baking powder
- 2 eggs
- 4 1/2 cups all-purpose flour
- 6 tablespoons orange juice
- 1 (12 ounce) can poppyseed filling

DIRECTIONS

1. In a large bowl, cream together the butter and sugar until smooth. Beat in the eggs one at a time, then stir in the orange juice and vanilla. Mix in the baking powder, then gradually stir in the flour until the dough forms a ball. Cover and refrigerate at least 2 hours. I like to do mine overnight.
2. Preheat the oven to 375 degrees F (190 degrees C). Grease cookie sheets.
3. On a lightly floured surface, roll the dough out to 1/4 inch thickness. Cut into 3 inch circles using a cookie cutter or drinking glass. Place circles on the prepared cookie sheets. Spoon 1 teaspoon of filling onto the center of each circle. (Any more and it will ooze out) Pinch the sides of each circle to form a triangle, covering as much of the filling as possible. The cookies may be frozen on the cookie sheets if desired to help retain their shape while cooking.
4. Bake for 8 to 10 minutes in the preheated oven, until light golden brown. These are best undercooked slightly. Cool on the baking sheet for a few minutes before removing to wire racks to cool completely.

REINDEER COOKIES

Servings: 36 | Prep: 30m | Cooks: 10m | Total: 40m

NUTRITION FACTS

Calories: 208 | Carbohydrates: 25.9g | Fat: 10.2g | Protein: 4.5g | Cholesterol: 24mg

INGREDIENTS

- 1 cup butter, softened
- 1/2 teaspoon salt
- 1 cup white sugar
- 3 cups all-purpose flour
- 1 cup smooth peanut butter
- 2 teaspoons baking soda
- 2 eggs

- 72 small pretzel twists, or as needed
- 1 teaspoon vanilla extract
- ½ cup chocolate chips, or as needed

DIRECTIONS

1. Preheat oven to 375 degrees F (190 degrees C).
2. Beat butter, sugar, peanut butter, eggs, vanilla extract, and salt together in a bowl until smooth and creamy. Stir flour and baking soda into creamed butter mixture until well incorporated.
3. Roll dough into 36 balls. Flatten each ball and shape into an upside-down triangle. Press two pretzels into the two top corners of each triangle for the antlers. Press two chocolate chips into the center of each triangle for the eyes, and one chocolate chip or M&M on the bottom of the triangle for the nose. Arrange cookies on baking sheets.
4. Bake in the preheated oven until cookies are golden brown, 10 to 15 minutes.

RUM BALLS

Servings: 24 | Prep: 20m | Cooks: 5m | Total: 1h10m

NUTRITION FACTS

Calories: 148 | Carbohydrates: 22.3g | Fat: 4.9g | Protein: 0.9g | Cholesterol: 0mg

INGREDIENTS

- 1 (12 ounce) box vanilla wafer cookies (such as Nilla)
- 3/4 cup dark rum (such as Meyer's)
- 1 cup semisweet chocolate chips
- 1 cup confectioners' sugar, plus more for dusting
- 1/4 cup light corn syrup

DIRECTIONS

1. Place vanilla cookies in a food processor and process into fine crumbs.
2. Heat chocolate chips and corn syrup together in a saucepan over low heat. Cook, stirring often, until chocolate is melted and smooth, about 5 minutes. Remove from heat and stir in rum and confectioners' sugar until smooth. Fold in cookie crumbs; dough will be sticky.
3. Place saucepan in the refrigerator until dough is firm and easy to roll, about 15 minutes. Cover 2 plates with waxed paper; dust with confectioners' sugar.
4. Roll dough into 1-inch balls and place on the prepared plates. Dust rum balls with confectioners' sugar. Refrigerate until firm, about 30 minutes.
5. Remove rum balls from refrigerator and transfer to a resealable bag, including the extra confectioners' sugar. Seal the bag and shake to coat the rum balls completely with confectioners' sugar.

OATMEAL CHOCOLATE COCONUT MACAROONS

Servings: 15 | Prep: 15m | Cooks: 5m | Total: 20m

NUTRITION FACTS

Calories: 228 | Carbohydrates: 37.7g | Fat: 8.6g | Protein: 2.2g | Cholesterol: 17mg

INGREDIENTS

- 2 cups quick-cooking oats
- 2 cups white sugar
- 1 cup shredded coconut
- 1/2 cup butter
- 1/4 cup unsweetened cocoa powder
- 1/2 cup milk

DIRECTIONS

1. Mix oats, coconut, and cocoa powder together in a bowl.
2. Bring sugar, butter, and milk to a boil in saucepan, stirring occasionally; remove immediately from heat and stir into oat mixture.
3. Drop 15 spoonfuls of batter onto a sheet of waxed paper. Cool to room temperature before serving.

GLUTEN-FREE SUGAR COOKIES

Servings: 40 | Prep: 20m | Cooks: 10m | Total: 2h | Additional: 1h30m

NUTRITION FACTS

Calories: 88 | Carbohydrates: 9.8g | Fat: 5.4g | Protein: 0.5g | Cholesterol: 23mg

INGREDIENTS

- 2 1/2 cups gluten-free flour
- 2 eggs
- 1 teaspoon baking powder
- 1/4 cup cream cheese, softened
- 1/2 teaspoon salt
- 1/4 cup butter, softened
- 1 cup white sugar
- 1 teaspoon vanilla extract
- 3/4 cup butter, softened
- 1 1/2 cups confectioners' sugar
- 1 teaspoon vanilla extract

DIRECTIONS

1. Whisk flour, baking powder, and salt together in a bowl. Beat white sugar, 3/4 cup butter, and 1 teaspoon vanilla extract together in a bowl using an electric mixer; beat in eggs, 1 at a time, until mixture is smooth. Mix butter mixture into flour mixture and form dough into a ball. Wrap ball with plastic wrap and refrigerate for 1 hour.
2. Preheat oven to 325 degrees F (165 degrees C).
3. Roll dough onto a lightly floured surface and cut into shapes using cookie cutters. Arrange cookies on a baking sheet.
4. Bake in the preheated oven until edges begin to brown, about 10 minutes. Cool cookies on the baking sheet for 2 minutes before transferring to a wire rack to cool completely.
5. Beat cream cheese, 1/4 cup butter, and 1 teaspoon vanilla extract together in a bowl using an electric mixer until smooth. Slowly beat confectioners' sugar into cream cheese mixture until icing is smooth; spread onto cooled cookies.

OLD FASHIONED SUGAR COOKIES IN A JAR

Servings: 24 | Prep: 15m | Cooks: 0m | Total: 15m

NUTRITION FACTS

Calories: 180 | Carbohydrates: 24.5g | Fat: 8.2g | Protein: 2.2g | Cholesterol: 36mg

INGREDIENTS

- 3 cups all-purpose flour
- 1 cup butter, softened
- 1 teaspoon baking powder
- 2 eggs
- 1 teaspoon baking soda
- 1 teaspoon vanilla extract
- 1/8 teaspoon salt
- 1/2 teaspoon lemon extract
- 1 1/2 cups white sugar

DIRECTIONS

1. In a medium bowl, stir together the flour, baking powder, baking soda and salt; set aside. In a 1 quart large mouth jar, layer the sugar on the bottom and the flour mixture on top. Attach a tag with the following instructions:
2. Empty the contents of the jar into a large bowl. Cut in 1 cup of softened butter until the mixture is crumbly. In a separate bowl, beat 2 eggs, 1 teaspoon vanilla and 1/2 teaspoon of lemon extract until light and fluffy. Pour into the dry ingredients and mix until well blended. Cover bowl and chill for 1 hour.

3. Preheat oven to 350 degrees F (175 degrees C). On a lightly floured surface, roll the dough out to 1/4 inch in thickness. Cut into desired shapes with cookie cutters. Place cookies 1 1/2 inches apart onto cookie sheets.
4. Bake for 10 to 12 minutes in the preheated oven, until edges begin to brown. You can decorate them with sugar before baking of frost after baking.

GRANDMA'S RASPBERRY BARS

Servings: 24 | Prep: 20m | Cooks: 30m | Total: 50m

NUTRITION FACTS

Calories: 169 | Carbohydrates: 23.8g | Fat: 7.7g | Protein: 1.9g | Cholesterol: 15mg

INGREDIENTS

- 3/4 cup butter, softened
- 1/4 teaspoon salt
- 1/2 cup white sugar
- 3/4 cup raspberry jam
- 1/2 cup brown sugar
- 1 1/2 cups rolled oats
- 1 1/2 cups all-purpose flour
- 1/2 cup chopped walnuts
- 1 teaspoon baking powder

DIRECTIONS

1. Preheat oven to 350 degrees F (175 degrees C). Grease a 9x13 inch baking dish.
2. In a medium bowl combine butter, white sugar, brown sugar, flour, baking powder and salt; mix well. Spread 2/3 of mixture into prepared pan.
3. Spread jam over mixture.
4. Combine remaining mixture with oats and walnuts; sprinkle over jam layer.
5. Bake in preheated oven for 30 minutes.

WORKING MOM'S HAMENTASHEN

Servings: 24 | Prep: 10m | Cooks: 15m | Total: 30m | Additional: 5m

NUTRITION FACTS

Calories: 155 | Carbohydrates: 29.9g | Fat: 3g | Protein: 2.1g | Cholesterol: 16mg

INGREDIENTS

- 1 (18.25 ounce) package moist yellow cake mix

- 2 tablespoons water
- 1 cup all-purpose flour
- 1 cup fruit preserves, any flavor
- 2 eggs

DIRECTIONS

1. Preheat the oven to 375 degrees F (190 degrees C). Grease cookie sheets.
2. In a large bowl, mix together the cake mix and flour. Stir in the eggs and water to form a stiff dough. On a lightly floured surface, roll the dough out to 1/8 inch thickness. Cut into 3 inch round circles and place 2 inches apart onto the prepared cookie sheets. Place a teaspoon of filling into the center of each cookie and pinch the sides to form three corners. Moisten with water if necessary.
3. Bake for 6 to 8 minutes in the preheated oven, or until lightly browned. Allow cookies to cool for 1 minute on the cookie sheets before removing to wire racks to cool completely.

COOKIE MIX IN A JAR

Servings: 24 | Prep: 20m | Cooks: 0m | Total: 20m

NUTRITION FACTS

Calories: 139 | Carbohydrates: 27.7g | Fat: 3.3g | Protein: 1.5g | Cholesterol: 0mg

INGREDIENTS

- 1 cup packed brown sugar
- 2 cups all-purpose flour
- 1/2 cup white sugar
- 1 teaspoon salt
- 1 1/2 cups semisweet chocolate chips
- 1 teaspoon baking soda

DIRECTIONS

1. Mix the salt and baking soda with the flour, then layer the ingredients into a 1 quart, wide mouth jar. Use scissors to cut a 9 inch-diameter circle from calico. Place over lid, and secure with rubber band. Tie on a raffia or ribbon bow to cover rubber band.

CAPPUCCINO BROWNIES

Servings: 72 | Prep: 30m | Cooks: 35m | Total: 9h5m | Additional: 8h

NUTRITION FACTS

Calories: 127 | Carbohydrates: 16.4g | Fat: 6.9g | Protein: 1.6g | Cholesterol: 27mg

INGREDIENTS

- 2 pounds milk chocolate chips
- 3 tablespoons vanilla extract
- 1/4 cup instant coffee granules
- 1 teaspoon ground cinnamon
- 1 cup unsalted butter, softened
- 1 teaspoon salt
- 2 cups white sugar
- 2 cups all-purpose flour
- 8 eggs

DIRECTIONS

1. Preheat the oven to 375 degrees F (190 degrees C). Grease and flour four 8x8-inch baking pans.
2. Place the chocolate chips and the coffee granules in a double boiler over simmering water. Cook over medium heat, stirring occasionally, until melted and smooth. Set aside.
3. In a large bowl, cream the butter and sugar together until light and fluffy. Beat in the eggs two at a time, mixing well after each addition. Stir in vanilla, cinnamon, and salt, then mix in the melted chocolate. Mix in flour until just blended. Divide the batter equally into the prepared pans, and spread smooth.
4. Bake for 35 minutes in preheated oven, or until the edges pull from the sides of the pans. Cool on a wire rack. Cover, and refrigerate for 8 hours. Cut the cold brownies into bars to serve.

SANTA'S CHOCOLATE THUMBPRINT COOKIES
Servings: 24 | Prep: 1h15m | Cooks: 8m | Total: 2h | Additional: 37m

NUTRITION FACTS

Calories: 282 | Carbohydrates: 38.7g | Fat: 13.4g | Protein: 3.5g | Cholesterol: 32mg

INGREDIENTS

- 1 cup butter, softened
- 1/2 cup unsweetened cocoa powder
- 3/4 cup white sugar
- 1/2 teaspoon baking soda
- 3/4 cup corn syrup
- 1/4 teaspoon ground cinnamon
- 1 egg
- 1 (11 ounce) package white chocolate chips
- 1 teaspoon vanilla extract
- 1 (1.4 ounce) bar chocolate covered English toffee, chopped

- 3 1/2 cups all-purpose flour
- 1 (4 ounce) jar maraschino cherries, halved

DIRECTIONS

1. Beat butter and 1/2 cup sugar in large bowl until well blended; stir in corn syrup, egg and vanilla. In a separate bowl, combine flour, cocoa and baking soda; gradually add this dry mixture to butter mixture. Blend well. Cover and refrigerate dough for 1 hour or until firm enough to handle.
2. Preheat oven to 350 degrees F (175 degrees C).
3. In a small bowl, combine remaining 1/4 cup sugar and cinnamon. Shape dough into 1 inch balls; roll each ball in sugar mixture and arrange on a cookie sheet. Using your thumb, make an indentation in center of each cookie.
4. Bake in a preheated 350 degrees F (175 degrees C) oven for 7 to 8 minutes or until just set.
5. Remove the cookies from the oven. If the indentation has grown indistinct, use the top of a spoon and press indentation in further. Immediately place 1 teaspoon white chips into each indentation. After several minutes, swirl the melted chips with a spoon. Top with toffee bits and maraschino cherry halves (if desired). Cool cookies on a wire rack.

BETTY'S SUGAR COOKIES

Servings: 48 | Prep: 15m | Cooks: 30m | Total: 45m

NUTRITION FACTS

Calories: 80 | Carbohydrates: 9.1g | Fat: 4.5g | Protein: 0.9g | Cholesterol: 8mg

INGREDIENTS

- 1 cup shortening
- 2 1/4 cups all-purpose flour
- 1/2 cup white sugar
- 1/2 teaspoon baking soda
- 1/2 cup brown sugar
- 1/2 teaspoon salt
- 2 eggs
- 1/41 cup colored sugar for decoration
- 1 1/2 teaspoons vanilla extract

DIRECTIONS

1. Preheat oven to 350 degrees F (175 degrees C). Grease cookie sheets.
2. In a large bowl, cream together the shortening, white sugar and brown sugar until smooth. Beat in the eggs one at a time then stir in the vanilla. Combine the flour, baking soda and salt; blend into the creamed mixture. Roll dough into 1/2 inch balls and place them 1 inch apart onto the prepared cookie sheets. Flatten each ball slightly and sprinkle with colored sugar.

3. Bake for 8 to 10 minutes in the preheated oven. Allow cookies to cool on baking sheet for 5 minutes before removing to a wire rack to cool completely.

BROWN SUGAR CUT-OUT COOKIES AND ICING

Servings: 96 | Prep: 25m | Cooks: 6m | Total: 1h31m | Additional: 1h

NUTRITION FACTS

Calories: 75 | Carbohydrates: 9.3g | Fat: 3.9g | Protein: 0.7g | Cholesterol: 10mg

INGREDIENTS

- 1 cup butter, softened
- 1/4 cup milk
- 2 cups brown sugar
- 1 cup butter, very soft
- 1 teaspoon pure vanilla extract
- 1 teaspoon pure vanilla extract
- 5 cups all-purpose flour
- confectioners' sugar
- 1/2 teaspoon salt
- splash of milk
- 1 teaspoon baking soda

DIRECTIONS

1. In a large bowl, stir together 1 cup butter and brown sugar until smooth and creamy. Stir in 1 teaspoon vanilla. In a separate bowl, combine the flour, salt, and baking soda; stir into creamed mixture. Mix in milk, stirring until a soft dough forms. Cover, and chill for 1 hour.
2. Preheat oven to 365 degrees F (185 degrees C). On a floured surface, roll out dough to 1/4 inch thick. Cut into desired shapes using cookie cutters. Place cookies 2 inches apart on ungreased cookie sheets.
3. Bake in a preheated oven for 6 minutes. Cool on wire racks.
4. Meanwhile, in a large bowl, stir together 1 cup butter and 1 teaspoon vanilla until it becomes smooth and creamy. Gradually stir in sugar, one cup at a time, beating well after each addition. Beat in a splash of milk, and continue mixing until light and fluffy. Keep icing covered until ready to decorate. Spread icing on top of cookies.

CINNAMON PALMIERS

Servings: 24 | Prep: 20m | Cooks: 15m | Total: 1h | Additional: 25m

NUTRITION FACTS

Calories: 79 | Carbohydrates: 9.5g | Fat: 4.3g | Protein: 0.7g | Cholesterol: 1mg

INGREDIENTS

- 1/4 cup white sugar
- 3/4 teaspoon ground cinnamon
- 1 sheet frozen puff pastry, thawed
- 1/8 teaspoon ground cardamom
- 1 tablespoon butter, melted
- water
- 1/3 cup white sugar

DIRECTIONS

1. Sprinkle a flat work surface with 1/4 cup sugar; unfold puff pastry over sugar and roll out to a 15x10-inch rectangle. Brush pastry with butter. Mix 1/3 cup sugar, cinnamon, and cardamom in a small bowl; sprinkle evenly over buttered pastry.
2. Starting with a long edge of the pastry, roll pastry tightly around filling, stopping in the middle. Repeat with the opposite edge, meeting the first roll. Put a little water onto your finger and dot along the long edges that come together; press gently so the two rolled edges stay together. Refrigerate until slightly firm, 5 to 10 minutes.
3. Preheat oven to 375 degrees F (190 degrees C). Line a baking sheet with parchment paper.
4. Cut pastry into 1/4-inch slices. Arrange slices on prepared baking sheet about 1 inch apart.
5. Bake in preheated oven until golden and crisp, about 12 minutes. Allow cookies to rest on baking sheet for 1 minute before transferring to a wire rack to cool completely.

CHEF JOHN'S CHOCOLATE MINT BROWNIES

Servings: 16 | Prep: 10m | Cooks: 35m | Total: 1h15m

NUTRITION FACTS

Calories: 174 | Carbohydrates: 28.2g | Fat: 7g | Protein: 2.2g | Cholesterol: 39mg

INGREDIENTS

- 1/2 cup unsalted butter
- 1/4 teaspoon salt
- 1 1/8 cups sugar
- 2/3 cup all-purpose flour
- 3/4 cup unsweetened cocoa powder
- 1 cup powdered sugar
- 2 large eggs
- 2 tablespoons milk
- 1/2 teaspoon vanilla extract

- 1/4 teaspoon mint extract, or to taste

DIRECTIONS

1. Preheat oven to 325 degrees F (165 degrees C).
2. Melt butter in a small saucepan over medium-low heat.
3. Combine sugar and cocoa powder in a large bowl; stir in melted butter until mixture is smooth.
4. Stir in 1 egg, vanilla, and salt. Mix in second egg.
5. Fold in flour and transfer to ungreased 8x8-inch square baking dish.
6. Bake in the preheated oven for about 35 minutes.
7. Remove from oven and cool in the baking dish for 10 minutes before removing to cool completely on a wire rack.
8. Mix powdered sugar, milk, and mint extract in a bowl until smooth.
9. Pour icing over cooled brownies. Spread evenly and allow to set, about 30 minutes.
10. Slice into 16 brownies.

CHOCOLATE PRESS COOKIES

Servings: 45 | Prep: 20m | Cooks: 10m | Total: 30m

NUTRITION FACTS

Calories: 84 | Carbohydrates: 13.2g | Fat: 3.3g | Protein: 0.9g | Cholesterol: 4mg

INGREDIENTS

- 5/8 cup shortening
- 2 cups all-purpose flour
- 1 3/4 cups white sugar
- 6 tablespoons unsweetened cocoa powder
- 1 beaten egg
- 1/2 teaspoon salt
- 1/2 teaspoon vanilla extract
- 1/4 cup multicolored candy sprinkles (optional)
- 2 teaspoons milk

DIRECTIONS

1. Preheat the oven to 350 degrees F (175 degrees C).
2. In a medium bowl, cream together the shortening and sugar until smooth. Beat in the egg, and stir in vanilla and milk. Combine the flour, cocoa, and salt; stir into the creamed mixture until just blended. Fill cookie press, and press onto ungreased baking sheets. Decorate with sprinkles if desired.
3. Bake for 10 minutes in the preheated oven. Remove from baking sheets to cool on wire racks.

CHOCOLATE BALLS

Servings: 36 | Prep: 20m | Cooks: 15m | Total: 35m | Additional: 15m

NUTRITION FACTS

Calories: 121 | Carbohydrates: 12.9g | Fat: 7.8g | Protein: 2.5g | Cholesterol: 0mg

INGREDIENTS

- 1 cup peanut butter
- 2 cups semisweet chocolate chips
- 3/4 cup confectioners' sugar
- 3 (1 ounce) squares semisweet chocolate, chopped
- 1 cup graham cracker crumbs
- 1 tablespoon shortening

DIRECTIONS

1. In a medium bowl, mix together the peanut butter and confectioners' sugar until smooth. Stir in graham cracker crumbs until well blended. Form the dough into 1 inch balls by rolling in your hands, or by using a cookie scoop.
2. Melt the semisweet chocolate chips, semisweet chocolate squares, and the shortening in the top half of a double boiler. Use a fork to dip the balls into the melted chocolate, and place on wax paper to cool until set.

CHOCOLATE SNOWBALLS

Servings: 72 | Prep: 15m | Cooks: 20m | Total: 3h15m | Additional: 2h40m

NUTRITION FACTS

Calories: 74 | Carbohydrates: 6.1g | Fat: 5.5g | Protein: 0.8g | Cholesterol: 8mg

INGREDIENTS

- 1 1/4 cups butter
- 1/8 teaspoon salt
- 2/3 cup white sugar
- 1/2 cup unsweetened cocoa powder
- 1 teaspoon vanilla extract
- 2 cups chopped pecans
- 2 cups all-purpose flour
- 1/2 cup confectioners' sugar for decoration

DIRECTIONS

1. In a medium bowl, cream butter and sugar until light and fluffy. Stir in the vanilla. Sift together the flour, salt, and cocoa; stir into the creamed mixture. Mix in the pecans until well blended. Cover, and chill for at least 2 hours.
2. Preheat oven to 350 degrees F (175 degrees C). Roll chilled dough into 1 inch balls. Place on ungreased cookie sheets about 2 inches apart.
3. Bake for 20 minutes in preheated oven. Roll in confectioners' sugar when cooled.

SOUR CREAM SPRITZ

Servings: 96 | Prep: 20m | Cooks: 12m | Total: 35m | Additional: 3m

NUTRITION FACTS

Calories: 38 | Carbohydrates: 4.4g | Fat: 2.2g | Protein: 0.4g | Cholesterol: 8mg

INGREDIENTS

- 1 cup butter, softened
- 2 3/4 cups all-purpose flour
- 3/4 cup white sugar
- 1 teaspoon ground cinnamon
- 1 egg yolk
- 1/2 teaspoon salt
- 1/3 cup sour cream
- 1/2 teaspoon baking soda
- 1 teaspoon vanilla extract

DIRECTIONS

1. Preheat oven to 375 degrees F (190 degrees C).
2. Cream together butter and sugar. Beat in egg yolk, sour cream and vanilla. In a separate bowl, mix flour, cinnamon, salt and baking soda. Stir flour mixture into butter mixture. Place dough into a cookie press and press cookies onto ungreased baking sheets.
3. Bake in preheated oven 10 to 12 minutes, until golden. Cool 5 minutes on sheet before moving to wire rack to cool completely.

PERFECT DOUBLE CHOCOLATE PEANUT CANDY COOKIES

Servings: 48 | Prep: 30m | Cooks: 10m | Total: 1h25m | Additional: 45m

NUTRITION FACTS

Calories: 121 | Carbohydrates: 15.5g | Fat: 6.4g | Protein: 1.8g | Cholesterol: 13mg

INGREDIENTS

- 1/2 cup butter, softened
- 2/3 cup unsweetened cocoa powder
- 1/2 cup vegetable shortening
- 2 1/4 cups all-purpose flour
- 3/4 cup white sugar
- 1 teaspoon baking soda
- 2/3 cup packed brown sugar
- 1/4 teaspoon salt
- 1 teaspoon vanilla extract
- 3/4 cup semi-sweet chocolate chips
- 2 eggs
- 1 1/4 cups candy-coated peanut butter pieces (such as Reese's Pieces), divided

DIRECTIONS

1. Preheat oven to 350 degrees F (175 degrees C). Line baking sheets with parchment paper.
2. In a large bowl, beat the butter and shortening together with an electric mixer until well combined. Beat in the white and brown sugar until the mixture is creamy, then beat the vanilla extract and eggs, followed by the cocoa powder. Beat until the mixture is even in color. In another bowl, whisk together the flour, baking soda, and salt; stir the flour mixture into the cocoa mixture until the dough is thoroughly mixed. Stir in the chocolate chips and 3/4 cup of peanut butter candies. Reserve the rest of the candy pieces.
3. Cover the bowl with plastic wrap, and refrigerate the cookie dough until chilled, at least 45 minutes. Drop dough by tablespoon onto the prepared baking sheets. Gently press a few more candy pieces into the top of each cookie.
4. Bake in the preheated oven 8 to 9 minutes; cool on baking sheets for 1 to 2 minutes before finishing cooling on racks.

CHEWY NOELS

Servings: 18 | Prep: 15m | Cooks: 20m | Total: 35m

NUTRITION FACTS

Calories: 124 | Carbohydrates: 16.3g | Fat: 6.1g | Protein: 1.9g | Cholesterol: 24mg

INGREDIENTS

- 2 tablespoons butter
- 2 eggs, beaten
- 1 cup packed brown sugar
- 1 teaspoon vanilla extract

- 5 tablespoons all-purpose flour
- 1 cup chopped walnuts
- 1/8 teaspoon baking soda
- 1/4 cup confectioners' sugar for dusting

DIRECTIONS

1. Preheat oven to 350 degrees F (175 degrees C). Melt the butter in a 7x11 inch baking dish, and tilt the pan to coat all of the sides; set aside.
2. In a medium bowl, stir together the brown sugar, flour, and baking soda. Mix in the eggs and vanilla until smooth, then stir in the walnuts. Pour over the melted butter.
3. Bake in the preheated oven for 20 minutes, or until the edges begin to brown. Cool, then cut into squares, and dust with confectioners sugar.

PEPPERMINT BARS

Servings: 12 | Prep: 15m | Cooks: 25m | Total: 40m

NUTRITION FACTS

Calories: 428 | Carbohydrates: 61g | Fat: 20.2g | Protein: 3.4g | Cholesterol: 56mg

INGREDIENTS

- 1 cup butter
- 2 cups all-purpose flour
- 1 cup white sugar
- 1/4 teaspoon salt
- 1 egg
- 1 cup crushed peppermint candy canes, divided
- 1/4 teaspoon peppermint extract
- 1 cup semisweet chocolate chips
- 5 drops red food coloring

DIRECTIONS

1. Preheat oven to 350 degrees F(175 degrees C) and grease a 9x13-inch pan.
2. Cream butter and sugar. Beat in egg, peppermint extract, and food coloring. Add flour and salt till well blended. Stir in 2/3 cup finely crushed candy. Spread evenly into the greased pan.
3. Bake until firm, about 25 minutes.
4. After removing from oven, immediately sprinkle with chocolate chips. Cover with a cookie sheet for 1 minute or until melted. Spread chocolate evenly and sprinkle with 1/3 cup coarsely chopped candy. Cool completely before cutting.

CANDY CANE CHOCOLATE CHUNK COOKIES

Servings: 36 | Prep: 25m | Cooks: 10m | Total: 45m | Additional: 10m

NUTRITION FACTS

Calories: 144 | Carbohydrates: 19.2g | Fat: 6.7g | Protein: 1.7g | Cholesterol: 25mg

INGREDIENTS

- 1 cup butter, softened
- 1 teaspoon cream of tartar
- 1/2 cup white sugar
- 1 teaspoon baking soda
- 2 eggs
- 1/2 teaspoon salt
- 2 teaspoons vanilla extract
- 1 (5 ounce) milk chocolate candy bar, chopped
- 1/2 teaspoon peppermint extract
- 1 cup coarsely chopped peppermint candy canes
- 2 3/4 cups all-purpose flour

DIRECTIONS

1. Preheat the oven to 400 degrees F (200 degrees C).
2. In a medium bowl, cream together the butter and sugar until smooth. Beat in the eggs one at a time, then stir in the vanilla and peppermint extracts. Combine the flour, cream of tartar, baking soda, and salt; stir into the creamed mixture until all of the dry has been absorbed. Mix in the chocolate chunks and chopped candy cane. Form spoonfuls of dough into balls, and place them 2 inches apart onto an ungreased baking sheet.
3. Bake for 8 to 10 minutes in the preheated oven.

LEBKUCHEN

Servings: 72 | Prep: 20m | Cooks: 10m | Total: 10h | Additional: 9h30m

NUTRITION FACTS

Calories: 61 | Carbohydrates: 13.8g | Fat: 0.5g | Protein: 0.7g | Cholesterol: 3mg

INGREDIENTS

- 1/2 cup honey
- 1 teaspoon ground cloves
- 1/2 cup molasses
- 1 teaspoon ground allspice

- 3/4 cup packed brown sugar
- 1 teaspoon ground nutmeg
- 1 egg
- 1/3 cup diced candied citron
- 1 tablespoon lemon juice
- 1/3 cup chopped hazelnuts
- 1 teaspoon lemon zest
- 1 cup white sugar
- 2 3/4 cups all-purpose flour
- 1/2 cup water
- 1/2 teaspoon baking soda
- 1/4 cup confectioners' sugar
- 1 teaspoon ground cinnamon

DIRECTIONS

1. In a medium saucepan, stir together the honey and molasses. Bring the mixture to a boil, remove from heat and stir in the brown sugar, egg, lemon juice and lemon zest. In a large bowl, stir together the flour, baking soda, cinnamon, cloves, allspice and nutmeg. Add the molasses mixture to the dry ingredients and mix well. Stir in the citron and hazelnuts. Cover dough and chill overnight.
2. Preheat oven to 350 degrees F (175 degrees C). Grease cookie sheets. Using a small amount of dough at a time, roll out on a lightly floured surface to 1/4 inch thickness. Cut into small rectangles and place them 1 inch apart onto the prepared cookie sheet.
3. Bake for 10 to 12 minutes in the preheated oven, until no imprint remains when touched lightly. Brush the icing over the cookies while they are still hot and quickly remove them to wire cooling racks. Store in airtight container with a cup of orange or apple for a few days to mellow.
4. To make the icing: Combine the sugar and water in a small saucepan. Heat to between 234 and 240 degrees F (112 to 116 degrees C), or until a small amount of syrup dropped into cold water forms a soft ball that flattens when removed from the water and placed on a flat surface. Remove from heat and stir in the confectioners' sugar. If icing becomes sugary while brushing cookies, re-heat slightly- adding a little water until crystals dissolve.

CHEF JOHN'S ALMOND BISCOTTI

Servings: 15 | Prep: 15m | Cooks: 1h | Total: 2h

NUTRITION FACTS

Calories: 200 | Carbohydrates: 28.6g | Fat: 8g | Protein: 4.3g | Cholesterol: 31mg

INGREDIENTS

- 2 cups all-purpose flour
- 1 tablespoon olive oil

- 1 teaspoon baking powder
- 2 large eggs
- 1/4 teaspoon fine salt
- 1/4 teaspoon vanilla extract
- 3 tablespoons unsalted butter, room temperature
- 3/4 teaspoon almond extract
- 1 cup white sugar
- 1/2 cup whole roasted almonds
- 1 tablespoon white sugar
- 1/2 cup chopped roasted almonds

DIRECTIONS

1. Whisk flour, baking powder, and salt together in a mixing bowl.
2. Place butter, 1 cup plus 1 tablespoon sugar, olive oil in a separate mixing bowl. Mix together thoroughly until mixture has a creamy texture. Add 1 egg; mix into butter/sugar mixture. Whisk in 2nd egg, vanilla extract, and almond extract; whisk until smooth. Add flour mixture. Mix until flour is incorporated. Add whole almonds and chopped almonds; mix in evenly. Cover bowl with plastic wrap; refrigerate 30 minutes.
3. Preheat oven to 350 degrees F (175 degrees C). Line a rimmed baking sheet with a silicone mat.
4. Divide dough in half. Place each half on a length of plastic wrap and shape into a log. Wrap with the plastic wrap and press into a shape about 3 or 4 inches wide and about 1/2 inch high. Transfer both pieces to prepared baking sheet leaving about 3 or 4 inches of space between them to allow for spreading.
5. Bake in center of preheated oven until turning golden and a toothpick inserted into the center comes out clean, about 30 minutes. Let cool 15 minutes before slicing.
6. Reduce oven temperature to 325 degrees F (165 degrees C).
7. Cut each piece at a slight angle into 1/2- to 1 -inch thick slices with a serrated knife. Transfer pieces back to baking sheet in a single layer. Bake 12 minutes; remove from oven and flip pieces over. Return pan to oven and bake until biscotti are golden brown and crunchy, about 20 minutes.
8. Transfer biscotti to a cooling rack; let cool to room temperature.

SUGAR AND SPICE COOKIES

Servings: 50 | Prep: 20m | Cooks: 10m | Total: 2h | Additional: 1h30m

NUTRITION FACTS

Calories: 51 | Carbohydrates: 7.8g | Fat: 2g | Protein: 0.6g | Cholesterol: 9mg

INGREDIENTS

- 1 3/4 cups all-purpose flour
- 1/2 cup softened butter
- 1 teaspoon baking powder
- 1 cup packed brown sugar

- 1 teaspoon ground cinnamon
- 1 egg
- 1/4 teaspoon ground nutmeg
- 1/2 teaspoon vanilla extract
- 1 pinch ground cloves

DIRECTIONS

1. Mix the flour, the baking powder, cinnamon, nutmeg, and cloves together in a bowl.
2. Cream the butter and brown sugar together with an electric mixer in a large bowl until smooth; beat the egg and vanilla extract into the butter mixture. Add the flour mixture in small amount to the butter mixture, beating each addition until blended. Form the dough into a ball, wrap with plastic wrap, and refrigerate at least 1 hour or up to 3 days.
3. Preheat an oven to 350 degrees F (175 degrees C). Grease baking sheets.
4. Roll the dough out on a floured work surface with a rolling pin to about 1/8-inch thickness. Cut with 2-inch cookie cutters. Arrange the cut cookies onto the prepared baking sheets.
5. Bake in the preheated oven until the edges begin to brown, 10 to 12 minutes. Allow the cookies to cool on the baking sheet for 1 minute before removing to a wire rack to cool completely.

PEPPERMINT SNOWBALLS

Servings: 60 | Prep: 20m | Cooks: 10m | Total: 30m

NUTRITION FACTS

Calories: 111 | Carbohydrates: 18.1g | Fat: 4g | Protein: 0.8g | Cholesterol: 13mg

INGREDIENTS

- 3 cups confectioners' sugar
- 1 teaspoon baking powder
- 1 1/4 cups butter, softened
- 1/2 teaspoon salt
- 1 teaspoon peppermint extract
- 1 cup white sugar, or as needed
- 1 teaspoon vanilla extract
- 1 cup finely crushed peppermint candy
- 1 egg
- 3 tablespoons milk
- 3 cups all-purpose flour

DIRECTIONS

1. Preheat oven to 350 degrees F (175 degrees C). Lightly grease baking sheets, or line with parchment paper.

2. Beat 1 1/2 cups confectioners' sugar with the butter, peppermint extract, vanilla extract, and egg in a mixing bowl at Medium speed until well blended and creamy, 2 to 3 minutes. Reduce speed to Low, and gradually mix in the flour, baking powder, and salt until well blended, 1 to 2 minutes. Stir in 1/2 cup crushed peppermint candy using a wooden spoon.

3. Place the white sugar in a shallow bowl. Roll a small amount of cookie dough between your hands to make 3/4 inch diameter balls. Roll in sugar. Place 1 inch apart on prepared baking sheets.

4. Bake in preheated oven until light brown, 10 to 12 minutes. Remove and cool on racks.

5. Meanwhile, to make the glaze, stir the remaining 1 1/2 cups confectioners sugar together with the milk in a bowl until smooth. Drizzle cooled cookies with the glaze, and sprinkle immediately with the remaining crushed peppermint candy.

CHOCOLATE SANDWICH COOKIES

Servings: 12 | Prep: 30m | Cooks: 8m | Total: 1h10m | Additional: 32m

NUTRITION FACTS

Calories: 600 | Carbohydrates: 86.6g | Fat: 26.9g | Protein: 6.6g | Cholesterol: 64mg

INGREDIENTS

- 3 cups all-purpose flour
- 3/4 cup shortening
- 1 1/2 cups white sugar
- 3/4 cup butter, softened
- 3/4 cup unsweetened cocoa powder
- 2 cups confectioners' sugar
- 3/4 teaspoon salt
- 1/8 teaspoon salt
- 3 teaspoons baking powder
- 1 (7 ounce) jar marshmallow creme
- 1 1/2 cups milk
- 1 1/2 teaspoons vanilla extract
- 2 eggs
- 1 tablespoon milk
- 1 1/2 teaspoons vanilla extract

DIRECTIONS

1. Preheat oven to 400 degrees F (200 degrees C).

2. In a large bowl, combine flour, white sugar, cocoa powder, 3/4 teaspoon salt, and baking powder. Stir in 1 1/2 cups milk, eggs, 1 1/2 teaspoons vanilla, and shortening. Mix until smooth using an electric mixer. Drop batter by rounded teaspoons onto ungreased cookie sheets. Leave space, and only use a teaspoon; these spread.

3. Bake in preheated oven for 7 to 8 minutes. Remove from pan immediately, and cool on wire rack.
4. To make the filling, combine the butter, confectioners' sugar, 1/8 teaspoon salt, marshmallow creme, 1 1/2 teaspoons vanilla, and 1 tablespoon milk in a medium bowl. Beat with mixer until fluffy. Spread filling on one cookie, and top with another sandwich style.

HEDGEHOG COOKIES

Servings: 24 | Prep: 1h | Cooks: 10m | Total: 3h10m | Additional: 2h

NUTRITION FACTS

Calories: 280 | Carbohydrates: 34.2g | Fat: 15.2g | Protein: 3.4g | Cholesterol: 16mg

INGREDIENTS

- 4 cups all-purpose flour
- 1/4 cup corn syrup
- 3/4 teaspoon baking powder
- 2 eggs
- 1/2 teaspoon baking soda
- 1 tablespoon vanilla extract
- 1/2 teaspoon salt
- 1 cup pecans
- 1 1/4 cups white sugar
- 1 cup chocolate chips
- 1 cup butter-flavored shortening

DIRECTIONS

1. Mix flour, baking powder, baking soda, and salt in a bowl. Whisk sugar, shortening, corn syrup, eggs, and vanilla extract in a separate bowl. Stir sugar mixture into flour mixture until just combined. Refrigerate dough until chilled, 30 minutes to 1 hour.
2. Preheat oven to 350 degrees F (175 degrees C).
3. Scoop cookie dough using a cookie scoop or 1 tablespoon so all the cookies are uniform; shape dough into teardrop-shaped cookies. Flatten the pointed side of each cookie to form the 'face'. Arrange cookies on baking sheets.
4. Bake in the preheated oven until golden, 10 to 12 minutes. Cool on the baking sheets for 10 minutes before removing to cool completely on a wire rack.
5. Pulse pecans in a food processor until finely chopped; transfer to a bowl.
6. Melt chocolate chips in the top of a double boiler over simmering water, stirring frequently and scraping down the sides with a rubber spatula to avoid scorching.
7. Dip the top of each cookie in the melted chocolate, spreading to fully coat the 'body' of each hedgehog. Press cookies, chocolate-side down, into the ground pecans forming the 'fur'. Arrange cookies on a sheet of waxed paper to set, about 30 minutes.

8. Transfer the remaining melted chocolate to a piping bag or plastic bag with a corner snipped. Pipe chocolate onto the pointed end of each cookie for eyes and a nose.

GINGERBREAD COOKIE MIX IN A JAR

Servings: 18 | Prep: 20m | Cooks: 0m | Total: 20m

NUTRITION FACTS

Calories: 137 | Carbohydrates: 31g | Fat: 0.3g | Protein: 2.6g | Cholesterol: 0mg

INGREDIENTS

- 2 cups all-purpose flour
- 1 teaspoon ground cloves
- 1 teaspoon baking powder
- 1 teaspoon ground cinnamon
- 1 teaspoon baking soda
- 1 teaspoon ground allspice
- 1 1/2 cups all-purpose flour
- 1 cup packed brown sugar
- 2 teaspoons ground ginger

DIRECTIONS

1. Mix 2 cups of the flour with the baking soda and baking powder. Mix the remaining 1 1/2 cups flour with the ginger, cloves, cinnamon, and allspice. In a 1 quart, wide mouth canning jar, layer the ingredients starting with the flour and baking powder mixture, then the brown sugar, and finally the flour and spice mixture. Pack firmly between layers.
2. Attach a card to the jar with the following directions: Gingerbread Cookies 1. Empty contents of jar into a large mixing bowl. Stir to blend together. Mix in 1/2 cup softened butter or margarine, 3/4 cup molasses, and 1 slightly beaten egg. Dough will be very stiff, so you may need to use your hands. Cover, and refrigerate for 1 hour. 2. Preheat oven to 350 degrees F (175 degrees C). 3. Roll dough to 1/4 inch thick on a lightly floured surface. Cut into shapes with a cookie cutter. Place cookies on a lightly greased cookie sheet about 2 inches apart. 4. Bake for 10 to 12 minutes in preheated oven. Decorate as desired.

TYLER'S RASPBERRY THUMBPRINTS WITH WHITE CHOCOLATE GLAZE

Servings: 48 | Prep: 20m | Cooks: 15m | Total: 45m | Additional: 10m

NUTRITION FACTS

Calories: 122 | Carbohydrates: 19.3g | Fat: 4.3g | Protein: 1.8g | Cholesterol: 16mg

INGREDIENTS

- 1/2 cup butter, softened
- 1 teaspoon baking soda
- 1/2 cup sour cream
- 5 ounces white chocolate, chopped
- 1 cup white sugar
- 2/3 cup raspberry preserves
- 2 tablespoons milk
- 1 tablespoon butter
- 2 eggs
- 1/2 (1 ounce) square white chocolate
- 2 2/3 cups all-purpose flour
- 1 cup confectioners' sugar
- 2 cups rolled oats
- 2 tablespoons milk

DIRECTIONS

1. Preheat oven to 350 degrees F (175 degrees C).
2. In a large bowl, cream together the 1/2 cup butter and sugar until smooth. Blend in the sour cream, 2 tablespoons of milk and eggs. Combine the flour, oats and baking soda, gradually stir into the creamed mixture. Finally, stir in the chopped white chocolate. Drop by rounded spoonfuls onto the prepared cookie sheet. Using a finger or your thumb, press a dent into the center of each cookie. Fill the dent with a 1/2 teaspoon of raspberry preserves.
3. Bake for 8 to 10 minutes in the preheated oven. Allow cookies to cool on baking sheet for 5 minutes before removing to a wire rack to cool completely.
4. To make the glaze: Combine 1 tablespoon butter and 1/2 ounce white chocolate in a microwave safe bowl. cook on high, stirring every 15 seconds until smooth. Gradually beat in the confectioners' sugar and milk until icing is of a drizzling consistency. Drizzle over cooled cookies.

DELICIOUS CHRISTMAS COOKIES

Servings: 54 | Prep: 15m | Cooks: 9m | Total: 25m | Additional: 1m

NUTRITION FACTS

Calories: 100 | Carbohydrates: 13.2g | Fat: 4.8g | Protein: 1.3g | Cholesterol: 8mg

INGREDIENTS

- 1 1/2 cups graham cracker crumbs
- 1/2 cup butter, softened
- 1/2 cup all-purpose flour

- 1 1/2 cups sweetened, flaked coconut
- 2 teaspoons baking powder
- 2 cups red and green candy-coated chocolate
- 1 (14 ounce) can sweetened condensed milk

DIRECTIONS

1. Preheat oven to 375 degrees F (190 degrees C).
2. In a medium bowl combine graham cracker crumbs, flour and baking powder.
3. In a separate, large bowl combine condensed milk and butter; beat until smooth. Stir in graham cracker mixture, mixing well. Stir in coconut and chocolates.
4. Drop by rounded teaspoonfuls onto ungreased cookie sheets.
5. Bake in preheated oven for 7 to 9 minutes, or until lightly browned. Allow cookies to cool on baking sheet for 1 minute before removing to a wire rack to cool completely.

RUM SUGAR COOKIES

Servings: 48 | Prep: 20m | Cooks: 9m | Total: 2h30m | Additional: 2h1m

NUTRITION FACTS

Calories: 82 | Carbohydrates: 10.2g | Fat: 4.1g | Protein: 1.1g | Cholesterol: 18mg

INGREDIENTS

- 3 cups all-purpose flour
- 2 eggs
- 1/2 teaspoon baking soda
- 1 cup white sugar
- 1/2 teaspoon salt
- 1 teaspoon rum flavored extract
- 1/2 teaspoon baking powder
- 1/2 teaspoon almond extract
- 1 cup butter
- 1/8 teaspoon ground nutmeg

DIRECTIONS

1. Mix together flour, baking soda, salt, baking powder, and butter until the mixture resembles cornmeal.
2. Combine eggs, sugar, rum extract, almond extract, and nutmeg until well mixed. Pour the egg mixture into the flour mixture. Stir until well blended. Divide the dough into two equal halves. Refrigerate the dough for 2 hours.
3. Preheat the oven to 350 degrees F (175 degrees C).

4. Place dough on a lightly floured surface. Roll the dough out until it is 1/8 inch thick. Using a cookie cutter cut the dough into cookies (whatever shapes you please). Place the cookies on an ungreased baking sheet.
5. Bake in the preheated oven until the edges are golden, 7 to 9 minutes. Allow the cookies to cool on the baking sheet for 1 minute before removing to a wire rack to cool completely.

COCONUT JAYS

Servings: 24 | Prep: 20m | Cooks: 5m | Total: 2h25m | Additional: 2h

NUTRITION FACTS

Calories: 140 | Carbohydrates: 18.9g | Fat: 7.7g | Protein: 0.7g | Cholesterol: 10mg

INGREDIENTS

- 1/2 cup butter
- 2 (1 ounce) squares unsweetened chocolate, melted
- 2 cups confectioners' sugar
- 1 (10 ounce) jar maraschino cherries, drained (optional)
- 3 cups flaked coconut

DIRECTIONS

1. Melt butter in saucepan. Remove from heat. Add sugar and coconut. Mix well. Shape into balls.
2. Make indent in center of each and place on cookie sheet. Place half a maraschino cherry in indent. Fill with melted chocolate. Chill until firm. Store in refrigerator.

CHOCOLATE-DIPPED COCONUT MACAROONS

Servings: 24 | Prep: 20m | Cooks: 20m | Total: 1h5m

NUTRITION FACTS

Calories: 133 | Carbohydrates: 10.7g | Fat: 9.9g | Protein: 2g | Cholesterol: 3mg

INGREDIENTS

- 3/4 cup sweetened condensed milk
- 1 large egg white
- 1/4 teaspoon almond extract
- 3 cups shredded unsweetened coconut
- 1 1/2 teaspoons vanilla extract
- 1 (4 ounce) bar semisweet chocolate, chopped, or to taste
- 1/4 teaspoon fine salt

DIRECTIONS

1. Preheat the oven to 350 degrees F (175 degrees C).
2. Combine condensed milk, almond extract, vanilla extract, salt, and egg white in a bowl. Whisk until thoroughly combined. Add about 2 1/3 cups shredded coconut. Mix with a spatula until mixture is sticky and holds together. Form into balls using a sorbet scoop.
3. Roll balls in remaining coconut. Space macaroons evenly onto a silicone-lined baking sheet.
4. Bake in the preheated oven until golden, about 20 minutes. Let cool to room temperature, at least 20 minutes.
5. Meanwhile, place 3/4 of the chocolate in top of a double boiler over simmering water. Stir frequently, scraping down the sides with a rubber spatula to avoid scorching, until chocolate is melted, about 5 minutes. Remove from heat and stir in the rest of the chocolate until it melts.
6. Dip the base of each cooled macaroon about 1/8 inch into the chocolate. Place cookies, chocolate-side down, on parchment paper. Let chocolate harden completely.

CHOCOLATE PILE-UP COOKIES

Servings: 60 | Prep: 15m | Cooks: 10m | Total: 45m | Additional: 20m

NUTRITION FACTS

Calories: 133 | Carbohydrates: 14.8g | Fat: 7.7g | Protein: 1.7g | Cholesterol: 16mg

INGREDIENTS

- 2 cups all-purpose flour
- 2 eggs
- 3/4 cup unsweetened cocoa powder
- 2 teaspoons vanilla extract
- 1 teaspoon baking soda
- 2 tablespoons coffee-flavored liqueur
- 1 teaspoon salt
- 1 cup finely chopped toasted hazelnuts
- 1 cup unsalted butter, at room temperature
- 1 cup semisweet chocolate chips
- 3/4 cup white sugar
- 1 cup milk chocolate chips
- 3/4 cup brown sugar
- 1 cup white chocolate chips

DIRECTIONS

1. Preheat an oven to 375 degrees F (190 degrees C). Line baking sheets with parchment paper. In a bowl, mix the flour, cocoa, baking soda, and salt.
2. Beat the butter, white sugar, and brown sugar together in a bowl with an electric mixer until soft and creamy, then beat in the eggs, vanilla extract, and coffee liqueur. Gradually beat the flour mixture

into the butter-sugar mixture until well combined. Stir in the hazelnuts, semisweet chocolate chips, milk chocolate chips, and white chocolate chips until evenly distributed through the dough. Drop by rounded teaspoons, about 2 inches apart, onto the prepared baking sheets.

3. Bake in the preheated oven until the edges are slightly browned, 8 to 10 minutes. Allow the cookies to cool on the baking sheet for 1 minute before removing to a wire rack to cool completely.

GOOEY CHERRY BARS

Servings: 36 | Prep: 20m | Cooks: 40m | Total: 1h

NUTRITION FACTS

Calories: 156 | Carbohydrates: 24.9g | Fat: 5.9g | Protein: 1.5g | Cholesterol: 22mg

INGREDIENTS

- 2 1/3 cups all-purpose flour
- 1 1/2 teaspoons baking powder
- 1/3cup white sugar
- 1 (10 ounce) jar maraschino cherries, drained and juice reserved
- 3/4 cup butter, softened
- 1/2 cup chopped walnuts
- 2 eggs, lightly beaten
- 2 1/2 cups confectioners' sugar
- 1 cup brown sugar
- 2 tablespoons butter
- 1/2 teaspoon vanilla extract

DIRECTIONS

1. Preheat oven to 350 degrees F (175 degrees C). Lightly grease a 9x13 inch baking dish.
2. In a medium bowl, mix flour, white sugar and 3/4 cup butter until crumbly. Press into prepared pan.
3. Bake in preheated oven 12 to 15 minutes, until light brown.
4. In a food processor, combine eggs, brown sugar, vanilla and baking powder and process until smooth. Pour in cherries and walnuts and pulse until just chopped and incorporated, but not pulverized. Pour over crust.
5. Bake 25 minutes, until center is set.
6. To frost, cream together confectioners' sugar with 2 tablespoons butter and 4 tablespoons cherry juice until fluffy. Frost cooled dessert and cut into bars.

ROSEMARY SLICES

Servings: 60 | Prep: 25m | Cooks: 10m | Total: 2h50m | Additional: 2h15m

NUTRITION FACTS

Calories: 37 | Carbohydrates: 0.6g | Fat: 1.7g | Protein: 0.6g | Cholesterol: 7mg

INGREDIENTS

- 1/2 cup butter, softened
- 3/4 cup all-purpose flour
- 3/4 cup white sugar
- 1 tablespoon finely chopped fresh rosemary
- 1 medium egg
- 1/2 teaspoon baking powder
- 1 cup whole wheat flour

DIRECTIONS

1. Beat the butter and sugar together in a bowl until creamy and smooth, and stir in the egg until well incorporated. Stir in the whole wheat flour, all-purpose flour, rosemary, and baking powder until well blended. Cut the dough into 2 equal-sized pieces, and shape each piece into a log about 1 1/4-inch in diameter. Wrap the logs in plastic wrap, and refrigerate at least 2 hours, or place in freezer for about 1 hour.
2. Preheat an oven to 350 degrees F (175 degrees C). Line baking sheets with parchment paper.
3. Cut the logs of dough into thin slices, 1/8 to 1/4-inch thick. Place the slices on the prepared baking sheets, and bake in the preheated oven until the cookies are set and the edges turn golden brown, 10 to 12 minutes. Cool for 1 minute on baking sheets before removing to wire racks to finish cooling.